The Fact Factory

The Fact Factory

A Supplement to *Childcraft— The How and Why Library*

World Book , Inc.
a Scott Fetzer company
Chicago

Staff

President
Robert C. Martin

Vice President, Publisher
Michael Ross

Vice President, Editor in Chief
Robert J. Janus

Consultants

Karol Bartlett
    Educator and Science Curator
    The Children's Museum of
        Indianapolis
    Indianapolis, Indiana

Damaris Koontz
    Media Specialist and Consultant
    Salem, Oregon

Ginger Davis Kranz
    Educator and Consultant
    Winona, Minnesota

Anne O'Malley
    Educator and Consultant
    New Trier High School
    Winnetka, Illinois

Editorial

Managing Editor
Maureen Mostyn Liebenson

Associate Editor
Sharon Nowakowski

Permissions Editor
Janet T. Peterson

Copy Editor
Irene B. Keller

U.K. Editor
Jeff Groman

Writers
Mary Feely
Mary Kayaian
Diana K. Myers

**Head of Indexing
Services**
David Pofelski

**Director,
Product Development
and Research Services**
Paul A. Kobasa

Researchers
Cheryl Graham
Nicholas V. Kilzer
Karen McCormack
Grace Mergenthaler

Art

Executive Director
Roberta Dimmer

Art Director
Wilma Stevens

Designer
Lucy Lesiak

Contributing Illustrator
Steven Mach

Contributing Designers
Mary-Ann Lupa
Sandy Newell
Ann Tomasic

**Senior Photographs
Editor**
Sandra Dyrlund

Photographs Editor
Marc Sirinsky

Product Production

**Director,
Manufacturing/Pre-Press**
Sandra Van den Broucke

Manufacturing Manager
Barbara Podczerwinski

**Senior Production
Manager**
Randi Park

Proofreaders
Anne Dillon
Roxanne Rakoczy

Text Processing
Curley Hunter
Gwendolyn Johnson

**For information on other World Book
products, call 1-800-255-1750, x2238,
or visit us at our Web site at
http://www.worldbook.com**

**For information on sales to schools
and libraries, call 1-800-975-3250.**

World Book, Inc.
525 West Monroe
Chicago, IL 60661

Library of Congress Cataloging-in-Publication Data
The fact factory: a supplement to Childcraft—the how and why library.
    p.   cm.
    Includes bibliographical references (p.) and Index.
    Summary: A collection of fun facts about a variety of subjects, including ani-
mals, plants, the Earth, space, and notable people throughout history.
    ISBN 0-7166-0699-2 (hc)
    1. Curiosities and wonders Juvenile literature. [1. Curiosities and wonders.] I.
World Book, Inc. II. Childcraft annual.
AG243.F25 1999
031—dc21   99-22290

Printed in the United States of America

1 2 3 4 5 6 7 8 9 05 04 03 02 01 00 99

Contents

People Facts   76

Extreme Facts   108

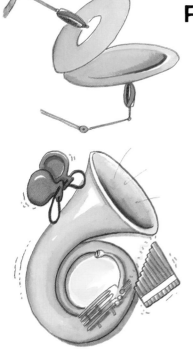

Preface

Welcome to *The Fact Factory*, the place that turns out all kinds of interesting facts. Some facts will make you laugh. Others may seem a bit scary. But all are geared to fascinate and inform you.

It's a fact that one animal's eye is bigger than its brain, but what animal is it? Where in the world does lightning strike most often? What is the fastest car in the world? What country makes the most movies? What plant shrivels up, looks dead, then seems to spring back to life once it gets water? The facts to answer all these questions are waiting for you inside, so get ready to start turning pages! And once you do, be sure to check out **From the Kid Fact Files**. This feature in each chapter fills you in on the facts about some very special young people.

Just in case you need a break from your fact-finding, there are games and activities sprinkled throughout each chapter. And at the back of the book, you'll find interesting words defined in the **Glossary**. You'll also find the **Index**, which lists what is in the book and on which pages it appears. Finally, other resources that are filled with interesting facts are listed in the section called **Find Out More**.

Have fun fact-finding! You may even find some facts that your teachers and parents don't know.

Have you heard of an animal that looks like a duck, except for the parts that look like a beaver? Did you know there is a plant that dries up and looks dead, and then springs back to life? Animals and plants include the strangest, the smartest, and the stinkiest things alive! They share your world, and fill it with wonder. That's a fact!

Incredible Animal and Plant Facts

Animal Antics

Hi, I'm Ann Emalpal. I am crazy about animals! So, when people here at the Fact Factory have a question about animals, they ask me. Why don't you help me answer my e-mail messages?

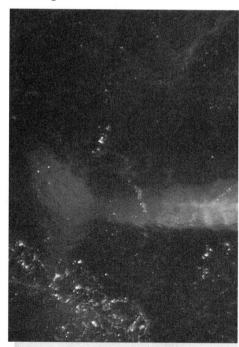

koalas

Q: Which kind of animal is the most common?

A: That's easy—bugs! Nobody has done an exact head count, but Earth has more insects than any other kind of animal. In fact, there are about 1 million insects for every human being!

Q: Which is the world's largest animal, the elephant or the giraffe?

A: Neither! The elephant is the biggest animal of the two, but the giraffe is the tallest. Some giraffes are as tall as three adults standing on each other's shoulders. But the elephant is the biggest animal that lives on land. The biggest of the big is the blue whale of the ocean. In fact, a blue whale is about as long as 30 8-year-old kids standing arm to arm!

The world's biggest animal, the blue whale, is about as long as 30 8-year-old kids standing arm to arm.

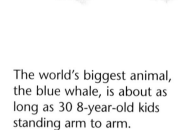

Q: Which animal likes to loaf around all the time?

A: The koala is one of the laziest animals. It stays awake for about two hours a day.

Q: Can you name an animal loudmouth?

A: No problem, the male howler monkey. You can hear the yell of a male howler monkey more than 3 miles (4.5 kilometers) away. In fact, he is the loudest land animal.

WHY is that?

The smartest animals, not counting humans, are baboons, chimpanzees, dolphins, elephants, gibbons, gorillas, monkeys, orangutans, pigs, and smaller-toothed whales. These animals are smartest because they can learn a number of tasks quickly and well. Also, each has a large brain compared with the rest of its body.

Q: How many kinds of animals are there?

A: Nobody knows. So far, scientists have found about 1 1/2 million kinds of animals. But many more may exist.

Q: Do scientists still discover new animals?

A: All the time! In the late 1990's, scientists found a new kind of monkey that is only 4 inches (10 centimeters) long. That's less than half the length of this page! This little monkey is called a dwarf marmoset (MAHR moh seht). It lives in a rain forest in Brazil.

In 1998, scientists found a worm living in a place that seems unbearable. The worm, called the Pompeii (pahm PAY) worm, lives on the ocean

Scientists discovered this little monkey in 1997. It's shown here at its actual size.

Riwoche horse

Round 'em up

Our efficient workers just sorted the animals. Which label should they give each group?

answers below

Animals	Group label
1. wolves	a. school
2. hares	b. litter
3. fish	c. pack
4. pigs	d. leap
5. frogs	e. pride
6. lions	f. troop
7. kangaroos	g. down
8. leopards	h. gaggle
9. whales	i. mob
10. monkeys	j. pod
11. geese	k. army

floor. Its home is a special tube near hot springs. The tube gets very hot, up to 176 °F (80 °C). Scientists do not know how the worm survives such heat!

Q: Have scientists found all the big animals?

A: Maybe, and maybe not. In 1995, scientists found a new kind of horse in Tibet. It's called the Riwoche (RUH woh chuh) horse. The horse is only about 4 feet (1 meter) tall at the shoulder. So maybe you are as big as a horse already. Scientists also found 200 Tibet red deer, an animal they thought had died out. Who knows what they will find next?

Tibet red deer

Answers: 1c; 2g; 3a; 4b; 5k; 6e; 7i; 8d; 9j; 10f; 11h

15

Q: What animal eats the yuckiest food?

A: Ooh, that's a hard one. One ultra-yucky meal is eaten by baby tarantula hawk wasps. (These wasps, by the way, are the official state insect of New Mexico.) First, a female wasp stings a tarantula spider. The sting paralyzes the spider. Then the wasp drags the spider to an underground nest. Finally, she lays an egg on it. When the egg hatches, the young wasp, called a larva, eats the spider alive—nibble by nibble. Yuck!

The tarantula hawk wasp stings a tarantula spider, then drags it home to feed her young.

Q: Do dolphins really talk to each other?

A: Yes. They send messages to each other by sounding out clicks and whistles, one after the other. They also send messages by slapping their tail fins, called flukes, on the water's surface.

Q: Do animals like to play?

A: Yes. For example, young gorillas in the wild love to wrestle. They also play games similar to Follow the Leader and King of the Mountain. And, they like to swing on vines. Do you think a gorilla would enjoy your favorite playground?

It's a baby!
The Fact Factory adopted several animal babies. Can you match each baby name with the animal or animals it describes? *answers below*

Baby name	Animal
1. kid	a. bird
2. bunny	b. horse
3. pup	c. kangaroo or koala
4. kitten	d. lion or shark
5. fledgling	e. skunk
6. calf	f. elephant or whale
7. joey	g. deer
8. fawn	h. rabbit
9. cub	i. goat
10. foal	j. dog or seal

Baby gorillas like to wrestle and play games.

Answers: 1i; 2h; 3j; 4e; 5a; 6f; 7c; 8g; 9d; 10b

Wanted: The Perfect Pet

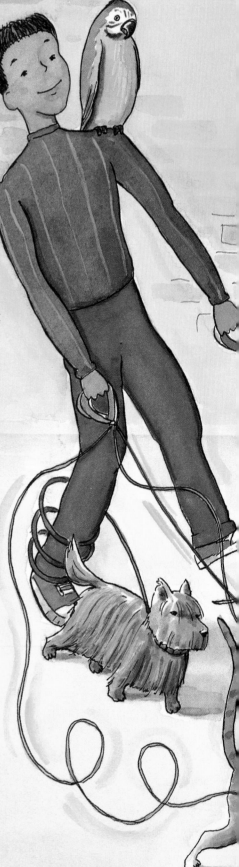

Here we are at the Fact Factory's Pet Department. I need to know more about pets because Mom and Dad say I am old enough now to get one. But what kind of animal would be best? Let's talk facts.

Dogs are great pals, but they need a lot of care and attention. Cats, on the other hand, are smart and loving, and easy to care for too. A cat would not mind being alone all day while I am at school. Hmm. This is a big decision.

Kids have had cats and dogs since early times. Fossils of pet dogs found in Israel and Iraq are about 12,000 years old. And the ancient

Oh, no!

Ferrets are probably the smelliest pets. This small animal is very smart. A ferret can learn to walk on a leash and use a litter box. But when a ferret gets excited, it gives off a strong odor from scent glands—just like its cousin, the skunk!

Egyptians loved cats. Some cats were made into mummies when they died!

There is one cute little creature called a mongoose. If I lived in India, I might get a mongoose. This small animal is famous because it moves so fast. It can pounce on a snake, even a poisonous snake, and kill it.

On the other hand, mice seem to make good pets. Kids in Japan like to keep mice. Mice are smart, gentle, and they don't take up much room. Some Japanese kids train their mice to dance!

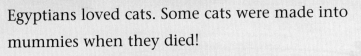

WHY is that?

Dalmatian dogs are favorite pets in fire stations. That is because Dalmatians used to work with firefighters. In the early 1900's, the fire engines were pulled by horses. Dalmatians ran ahead of the horses, barking like crazy. They warned people to get out of the way. Firefighters do not need Dalmatians to do this today, but they still love their old buddies!

Animal "Inventors"

Hi, it's me, Zack Leigh So! What do you think of when you hear the word *inventor?* A Stone Age person making the first wheel? A modern scientist finding a new cure? It is a fact that human beings have invented many marvelous things over the years. But we are not the only inventors. Animals invent things, too. Here are just a few of the inventions being displayed by animals.

Just as you carefully take medicine, chimps eat aspila leaves one at a time to keep healthy.

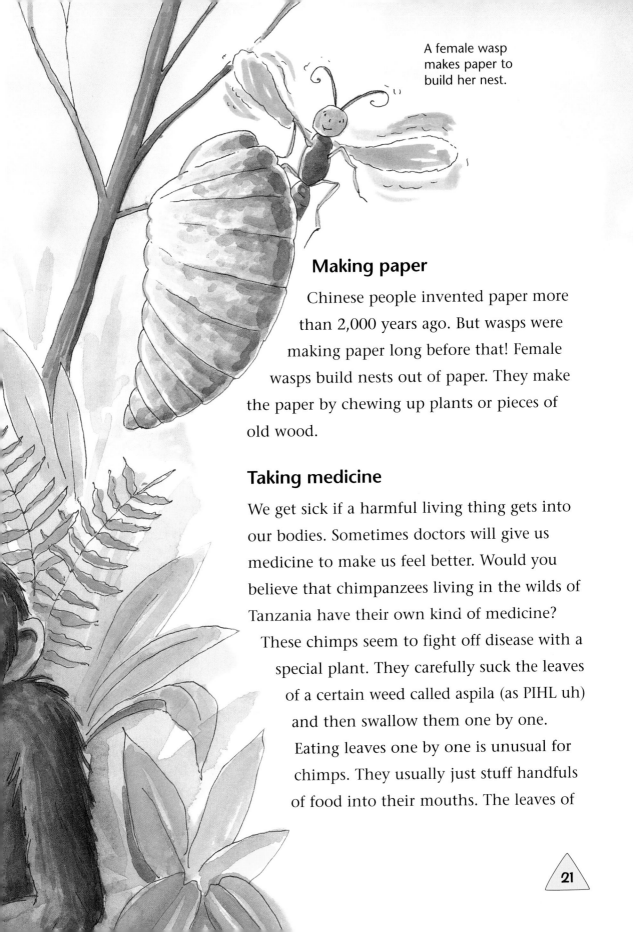

A female wasp makes paper to build her nest.

Making paper

Chinese people invented paper more than 2,000 years ago. But wasps were making paper long before that! Female wasps build nests out of paper. They make the paper by chewing up plants or pieces of old wood.

Taking medicine

We get sick if a harmful living thing gets into our bodies. Sometimes doctors will give us medicine to make us feel better. Would you believe that chimpanzees living in the wilds of Tanzania have their own kind of medicine?

These chimps seem to fight off disease with a special plant. They carefully suck the leaves of a certain weed called aspila (as PIHL uh) and then swallow them one by one. Eating leaves one by one is unusual for chimps. They usually just stuff handfuls of food into their mouths. The leaves of this weed contain a medicine that kills harmful living things. It knocks out bacteria (bak TEER ee uh), worms, and yeast. The chimps chew the leaves to get at their medicine.

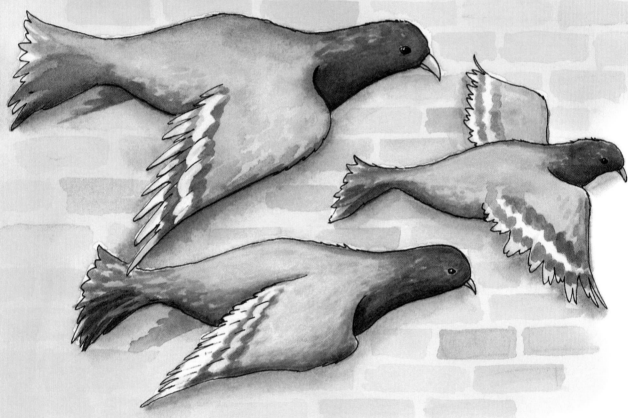

Many birds fly south for the winter. They use their built-in compasses to find the way.

Using a compass

You can find your way around with a compass because its needle always points north. The needle does this because it is really a magnet. Some animals that travel over long distances also use "compasses." Tiny magnets inside their bodies help them move in the right direction. Some of the animals that use compasses are insects, birds, and fish.

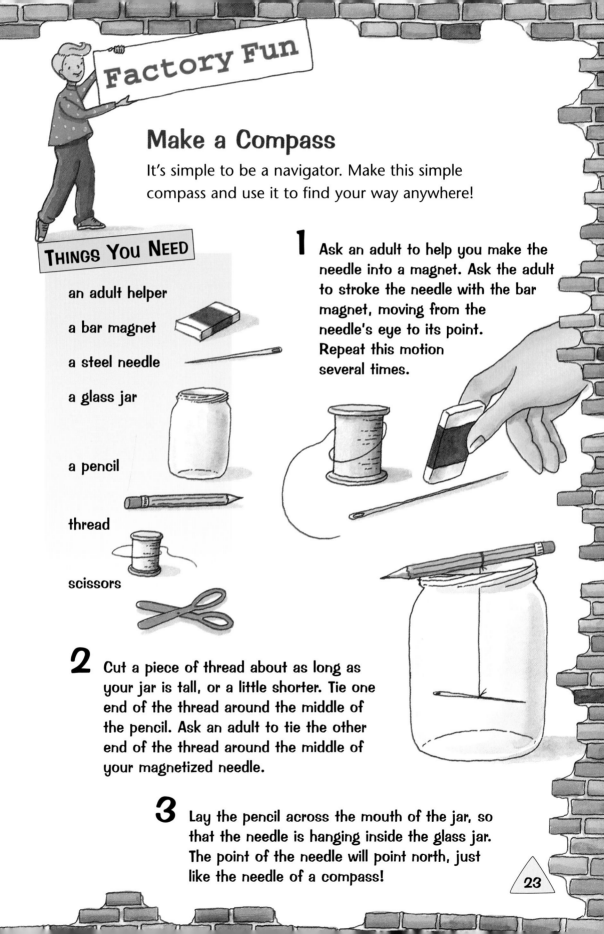

Factory Fun

Make a Compass

It's simple to be a navigator. Make this simple compass and use it to find your way anywhere!

1 Ask an adult to help you make the needle into a magnet. Ask the adult to stroke the needle with the bar magnet, moving from the needle's eye to its point. Repeat this motion several times.

2 Cut a piece of thread about as long as your jar is tall, or a little shorter. Tie one end of the thread around the middle of the pencil. Ask an adult to tie the other end of the thread around the middle of your magnetized needle.

3 Lay the pencil across the mouth of the jar, so that the needle is hanging inside the glass jar. The point of the needle will point north, just like the needle of a compass!

Seen a Mythical Creature Lately?

Hi, it's me, Ann Emalpal again. This is a really cool part of the Fact Factory, where myths (mihths) come to life! Myths are ancient stories that try to explain the world. Many, such as Greek myths, tell of fantastic creatures. One such creature was a bird called the phoenix (FEE nihks). This bird would burn itself up at the end of its life, and then a new phoenix would rise from the ashes.

phoenix

Another fabled creature was the Minotaur (MIHN uh tawr). It had the head of a bull and the body of a man. Pegasus (PEHG uh suhs), another famous creature, was a horse with wings.

Minotaur

Pegasus

Today we know that the phoenix, the Minotaur, and Pegasus were only myths

and never really existed. But you have probably seen animals that people once thought were myths that turned out to be real. Keep reading to find out about some of these creatures.

The awesome camelopard

One European could not believe his eyes when he visited Istanbul, Turkey, in 1599. There he saw "a strange and wonderful beast. . . . It has a long neck like a camel and is spotted like a panther." He and others thought the animal must be part camel and part leopard. They called it the camelopard. Have you ever seen a camelopard? Maybe you have. Today we call it a giraffe!

Eggs-traordinary!
The only other mammal that lays eggs like the platypus is the echidna (ih KIHD nuh), also called the spiny anteater. The mother echidna carries the egg in a pouch. After the egg hatches, the baby echidna stays in the pouch for several weeks. Echidnas live in Australia and New Guinea. The echidna scoops up its food—ants and termites—with its long, sticky tongue.

A duck with fur?

It sounds like somebody made it up. Explorers in Australia 200 years ago described it as part duck and part beaver. They said the creature had the bill and webbed feet of a duck, but the fur and tail of a beaver. Its young hatched out of eggs. But the mother fed the babies milk from its body, which no duck has ever done! When explorers brought the skin of this bizarre beast back to England in 1798, people were sure it was a fake.

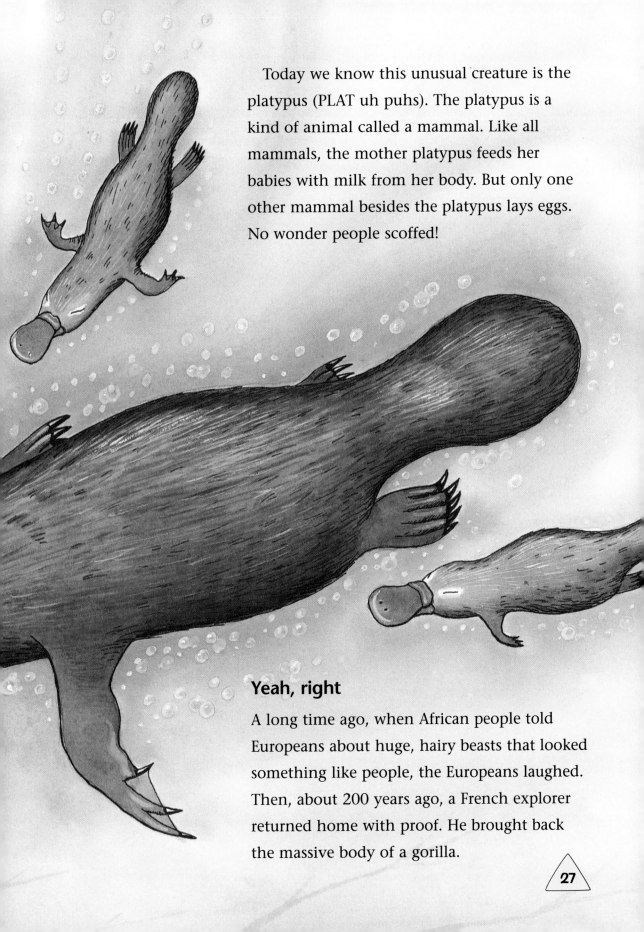

Today we know this unusual creature is the platypus (PLAT uh puhs). The platypus is a kind of animal called a mammal. Like all mammals, the mother platypus feeds her babies with milk from her body. But only one other mammal besides the platypus lays eggs. No wonder people scoffed!

Yeah, right

A long time ago, when African people told Europeans about huge, hairy beasts that looked something like people, the Europeans laughed. Then, about 200 years ago, a French explorer returned home with proof. He brought back the massive body of a gorilla.

27

Could this, the world's largest lizard, have been mistaken for a fire-breathing dragon?

Big mouth, hot breath

Of course, some creatures are still legends. Tales of fire-breathing dragons, for example, may have been inspired by the crocodile. On hot days, the crocodile lies on land with its huge mouth stretched wide open. Hot air steams out. Could this be the fire-breathing dragon of the legends?

Or perhaps the legends grew from sightings of the world's largest lizard, the Komodo (kuh MOH doh) dragon of Indonesia. This lizard may grow over 10 feet (3 meters) long. It shoots its long, yellow-pink tongue in and out of its mouth. Maybe this flicking tongue looked like a flame. And maybe people didn't hang around for a second look! What do you think?

Bee, I'm Expecting You!

by Emily Dickinson

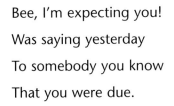

Bee, I'm expecting you!
Was saying yesterday
To somebody you know
That you were due.

The frogs got home last week,
Are settled and at work,
Birds mostly back,
The clover warm and thick.

You'll get my letter by
The seventeenth; reply,
Or better, be with me.
Yours,
Fly.

Emily Dickinson

Emily Dickinson was a shy person, but she loved the natural world. Many of her poems describe the plants and animals that grew near her home in Massachusetts. Emily also had a gentle sense of humor, as you can see from this poem. Today, we know that Emily was one of America's greatest poets.

From the Kid Fact Files

Name: Mary Anning

Home: Lyme Regis, England

Birthdate: 1799

Claim to Fame: Fossil finder

From the Kid Fact Files comes this story of a young girl who made a surprising animal discovery, and then many more.

Mary Anning could not believe what her brother Joseph had carried home. It was a huge skull more than 2 feet (60 centimeters) long. The 11-year-old girl and her brother loved digging fossils out of the sea cliffs near their home. But they had never found a fossil this big! They decided the skull belonged to an ancient crocodile. They searched for the rest of the skeleton, but they could not find it.

One night, a fierce storm blew up. The next morning, when all was calm, Mary went to the beach. Massive bones were sticking out of the cliff! Mary realized that the wind had uncovered the rest of the crocodile fossil. She asked some people to help her dig it out and carry it home.

The news about the huge fossil traveled fast. Scientists came to see it. They said it was not a crocodile at all. It was an ichthyosaur (IHK thee uh sawr). This fishlike lizard lived during the time of the dinosaurs. Mary had found the first complete skeleton of an ichthyosaur!

A rich man bought the skeleton and gave it to a museum. Mary's family was very poor, but now they could move into a nice home. As an adult, Mary made more discoveries. She found a skeleton of a plesiosaurus (PLEE zee uh sawr uhs), an ancient sea serpent, and the fossil of a pterodactyl (ter uh DAK tuhl), a long-extinct flying reptile. And, Mary got a new name, "The Fossil Woman"!

Planter Banter

Howdy! Jack's the name. You may have heard of me. I am famous. I once grew a giant beanstalk from some tiny beans. Ever since then, plants have been my favorite things.

Now I work in the Fact Factory's garden. Let's stroll around, and I will show you why I am so goofy about greenery.

King's holly

Prehistoric plant

Right here is the world's oldest plant. It is called King's holly, and it grows in Tasmania, Australia. This plant is about 40,000 years old. That means it was here during the Stone Age!

titan arum

Pee-ew!

Yuck, time to hold our noses. This is the world's smelliest plant, the titan arum (TY tuhn AYR uhm). It grows in Sumatra, and it smells like rotting fish mixed with burned sugar! This plant is also one of the largest herbs. Its leaf can be 13 feet (4 meters) wide.

bamboo

Grow and groan

You have grown a lot since you were a baby of course. But did you ever *hear* yourself grow? Well, we have a plant that grows so fast you can hear it getting taller! It is a kind of bamboo that grows up to 4 feet (1 meter) a day. It may be taller than you are! It creaks and whines and moans with every inch.

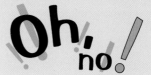

Oh, no!

The water hyacinth (HY uh sihnth) first grew in South America. There, its natural enemies, such as insects, kept the plant under control. But people brought the pretty plant to areas where it has no enemies. Today, the water hyacinth is probably the world's worst water weed. It clogs rivers and lakes, killing other plants and fish.

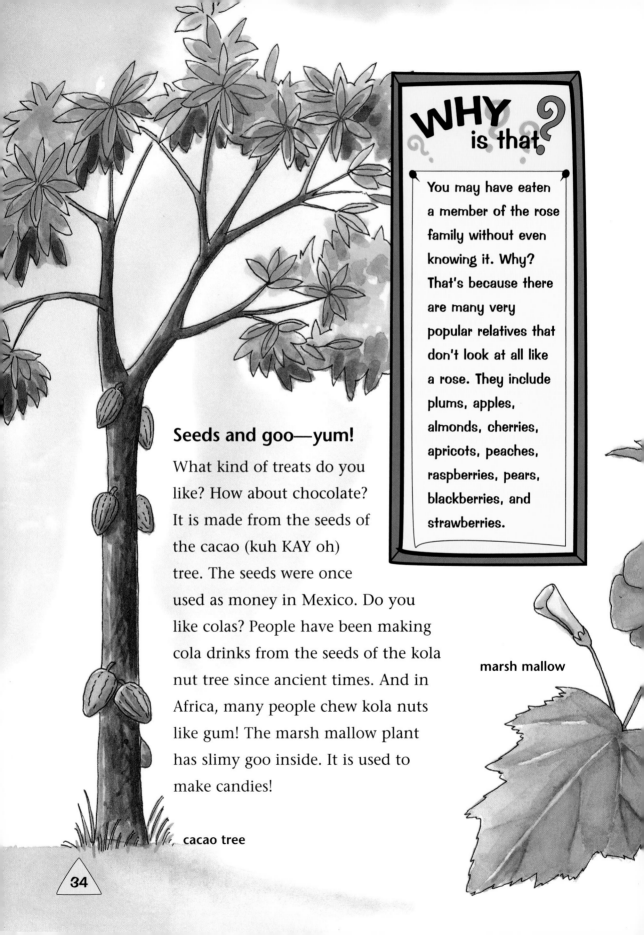

Seeds and goo—yum!

What kind of treats do you like? How about chocolate? It is made from the seeds of the cacao (kuh KAY oh) tree. The seeds were once used as money in Mexico. Do you like colas? People have been making cola drinks from the seeds of the kola nut tree since ancient times. And in Africa, many people chew kola nuts like gum! The marsh mallow plant has slimy goo inside. It is used to make candies!

marsh mallow

cacao tree

When brown and shriveled, a resurrection plant looks dead.

But give the plant some water, and it unrolls and turns green again!

Here to stay

The resurrection (rehz uh REHK shuhn) plant might look dead when it's all shriveled and brown. But don't worry. It is just thirsty. Water the plant, and it unrolls. Then it turns green again and starts growing!

Bizarre berries
A berry is a fleshy fruit with many seeds. Believe it or not, these foods are actually berries: bananas, white and black pepper (dried berries), watermelons.

cacao pod

cacao seeds

Bugs beware!

Most plants make their own food, but the pitcher plant likes meat! Its leaves are shaped like a pitcher. Rainwater collects in the pitcher. Its sweet, colorful "rim" attracts insects. Any bug that lands on the rim slides into the slippery "pitcher" and drowns in the water. Then, the plant eats it!

Welwitschia plant

pitcher plant

WHY is that?

Why can the soapberry tree come in handy at bath time? It can because its leaves and fruit make soapy suds when wet. In the tropical places where the tree grows, such as Asia and South America, people often use the plant as soap!

Big and sloppy

The Welwitschia (wehl WIHCH ee uh) plant has two large, leathery leaves. Each is a few feet wide and twice as long. But you may not know that by just glancing at the plant. In the African desert where it lives, the hot winds and blowing sand tear the leaves into ribbonlike shreds. In fact, it continues to grow slowly, and may live up to 2,000 years.

cereus cactus

Blooms for bats

Most flowering plants rely on insects to carry their pollen to other flowers. But the white flowers of the cereus (SIR ee uhs) cactus open only at night. Its pollen is spread by bats! The flowers are strong enough for a bat to hook onto with its claws!

Fact Factory Menu

Dear Customer:

Here at the Fact Factory cafeteria we like a lively menu. That's why we serve food from all over the world. Some dishes are vegetarian, and others are not. But all are delicious! Bon Appétit!

Starters

Bird's-nest soup

This delicious soup is made from the nests of swiftlets. Swiftlets are birds that hardly ever stop moving. They live in Asia. Swiftlets make their nests in a special way. The males use their saliva as cement to hold the twigs together. These nests make the soup nice and chewy!

China

Truffle

It is black, warty, and very pricey. Some people think it is very tasty too. The truffle is a kind of fungus. It grows underground, around the roots of oak, hazel, and other trees. Pigs love truffles. So, people use pigs to snuff out this fabulous fungus. Our highly prized truffle grows in France, Italy, and Spain. Order now. They won't last!

Spain

Italy

France

Entrees

Witchetty grubs

This dish is a favorite with Aborigine (AB uh RIHJ uh nee) kids in Australia. Witchetty grubs are the young larva of certain beetles and moths. They live in the ground, near the roots of certain plants. Do not miss a chance to taste this plump and juicy treat!

Australia

Haggis

Sink your teeth into the national dish of Scotland. First, we chop up the heart, liver, and lungs of a sheep. Then, we sprinkle in some animal fat called suet (SOO iht), along with onions, oatmeal, and seasonings. Finally, we cook it all together in a sheep's stomach.

Scotland

Side Dishes

Grass

Do you like rice, corn, wheat, oats, or millet? These are some of the world's favorite grain foods, and they come from plants in the grass family. So does sugar cane, which gives us sugar. Now, will you have one helping or two?

Oh, no!

Most people think of tomatoes, squash, and green peppers as vegetables. But these foods are fruits! And a peanut is not a nut at all. It is a legume (LEHG yoom), which is related to peas and beans.

Kelp

Tired of corn, carrots, and peas? Chew on this brown seaweed for a nutritious change. Kelp (kehlp) grows in cold seas and on rocky shores around the world. It is so popular in Japan and China that farmers grow it in special farms on the ocean. We serve kelp cooked or raw, and even powdered. You can sprinkle it on your food instead of salt!

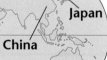

Japan

China

Dessert

Honeypot Ants

What a sweet surprise! These ants from Australia and Mexico are sweeter than honey. That's because they drink a sugary sap called honeydew from plants. Some ants drink so much honeydew that they swell up into tiny, living candies. For a taste sensation, toss a handful into your mouth or spread some on toast!

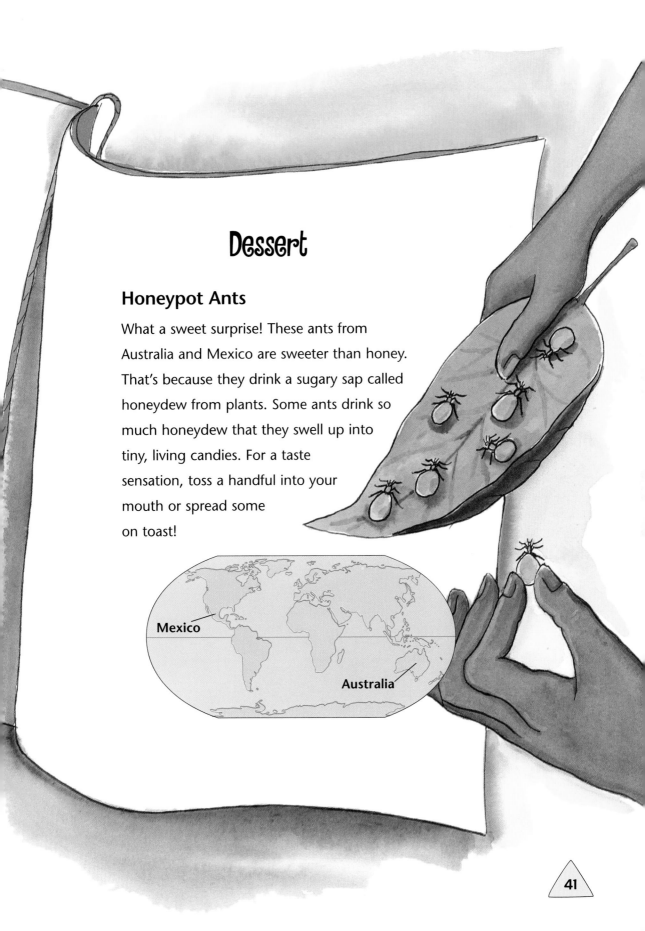

Mexico

Australia

Earth and Space Facts

Ancient pyramids reveal the past, while modern buildings reach for the sky. Mighty oceans heave on Earth, while towering volcanoes loom on Mars. Earth and space are full of wonders, and that's a fact!

Down to Earth Facts

Ssshhh! Zack Leigh So here. The Fact Factory's hectic today, so I'm taking off, literally! Up here, in my hot-air balloon, I can check some facts about our planet Earth.

The first thing you notice from up here is water, water, water, water! Oceans cover more than two-thirds of Earth.

The Pacific Ocean looks endless. This is the biggest ocean, with enough room for all of Earth's land! It is 488 times bigger than the largest lake, the saltwater Caspian Sea between Russia and several countries in Asia.

Can you name a river without water? Many of Australia's rivers are dry at least part of the year. The Darling River, Australia's longest river, is almost entirely dry during the winter!

At Asia's Dead Sea, people in the water completely float on their own, without inflatable tubes or rafts! The Dead Sea has the saltiest water anywhere. The sea is so salty that it holds a person up.

Australia

 **WHY is that?** It is easier to float in oceans and saltwater lakes than in fresh water. That is because salt water is more dense, or thick, so things float more easily. Check it out. Float an egg in a cup of fresh water, then start adding salt, keep adding lots. What eventually happens to the egg?

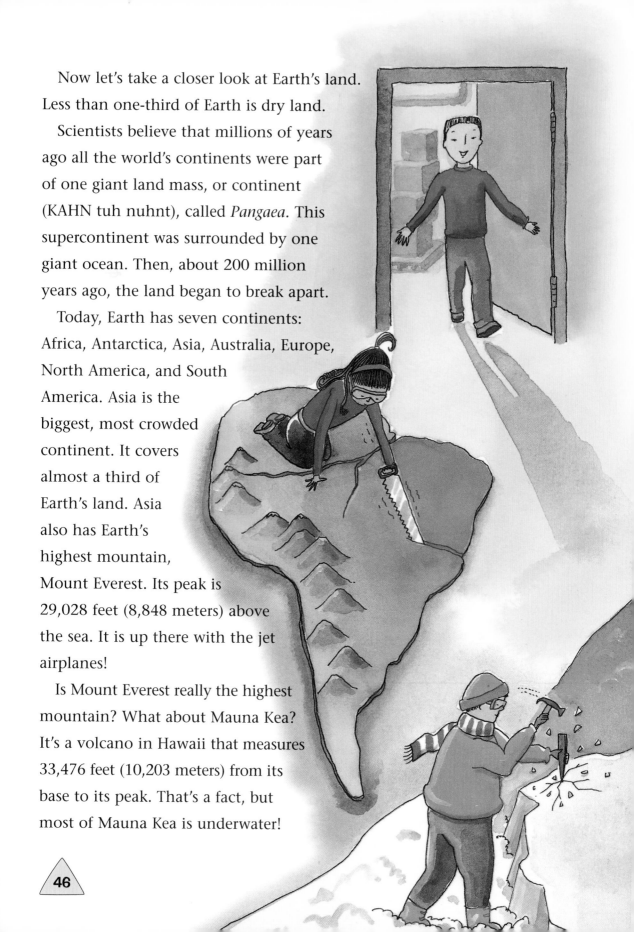

Now let's take a closer look at Earth's land. Less than one-third of Earth is dry land.

Scientists believe that millions of years ago all the world's continents were part of one giant land mass, or continent (KAHN tuh nuhnt), called *Pangaea*. This supercontinent was surrounded by one giant ocean. Then, about 200 million years ago, the land began to break apart.

Today, Earth has seven continents: Africa, Antarctica, Asia, Australia, Europe, North America, and South America. Asia is the biggest, most crowded continent. It covers almost a third of Earth's land. Asia also has Earth's highest mountain, Mount Everest. Its peak is 29,028 feet (8,848 meters) above the sea. It is up there with the jet airplanes!

Is Mount Everest really the highest mountain? What about Mauna Kea? It's a volcano in Hawaii that measures 33,476 feet (10,203 meters) from its base to its peak. That's a fact, but most of Mauna Kea is underwater!

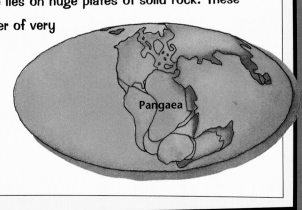

Earth's single giant continent was called *Pangaea* (pan JEE uh). It broke up because Earth's surface lies on huge plates of solid rock. These plates slide slowly on a layer of very hot rock. They move up to 4 inches (10 centimeters) a year—about as fast as your hair grows—causing giant earthquakes and volcanoes.

Pangaea

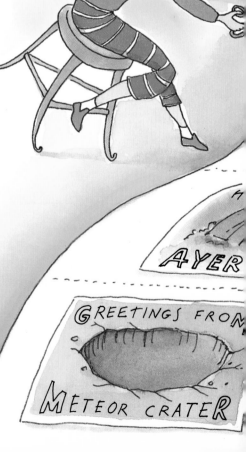

Some parts of Earth are so stupendous that people call them natural wonders. These seven natural wonders are particular favorites. Let's start at the top. There's Asia's towering Mount Everest. And the majestic Matterhorn, a mountain in Europe, is shaped like a pyramid.

Australia has two natural wonders. They are Ayers (AIRZ) Rock and the Great Barrier Reef.

Ayers Rock, or Uluru (oo loo ROO), is Earth's biggest rock. The rock is made of sandstone, and it seems to change colors. It ranges from pink to red to purple at sunrise and sunset, and black in the rain.

The Great Barrier Reef is Earth's longest group of coral reefs. The coral feels like rock, but it is actually made of the skeletons of tiny water animals.

Africa's Victoria Falls is a spectacular waterfall between Zambia (ZAM bee uh) and Zimbabwe (zihm BAH bway). The waterfall is about 1 mile (1.6 kilometers) wide. The roar of the waters is so loud that people named it *Mosi oa Tunya*, meaning "Smoke That Thunders."

AYER

GREETINGS FROM

METEOR CRATER

The United States has two natural wonders of the world. The Grand Canyon, in Arizona, is a valley about 1 mile (1.6 kilometers) deep and 277 miles (446 kilometers) long. Meteor Crater, also in Arizona, was dug by a chunk of iron that fell from space about 50,000 years ago. Ouch!

THE MATTERHORN

MOUNT EVEREST

ello from
S ROCK

The GREAT BARRIER REEF

VICTORIA FALLS

The BEAUTIFUL
GRAND CANYON

Mythical Cities Made Fact: Troy and Great Zimbabwe

Do you like getting your hands dirty? If so, then you'll want to spend time digging around this part of the Fact Factory. It has all kinds of facts about the incredible ruins of two long-ago cities, Troy and Great Zimbabwe.

The ruins of Troy are in what is now the country of Turkey. According to legend, Troy fought a war with Greece that lasted 10 years. We know about the war from a poem that is nearly 3,000 years old. This poem is called the *Iliad* (IHL ee uhd).

By the late 1800's, no one knew where Troy was. Some experts believed Troy was not real.

Oh, no!

Schliemann thought the eighth city was ancient Troy because he found treasure there. In fact, it turned out that the seventh city was Troy.

But a German businessman named Heinrich Schliemann believed it was. He started digging at a mound called Hissarlik, in Turkey.

Schliemann found several cities, one built on top of the other, and lots of gold treasure too. There were actually nine cities. The seventh city is probably Troy.

Another amazing ruin was once a thriving African city called Great Zimbabwe. Most of the granite blocks in its walls and buildings fit together without mortar.

One hundred years ago, some people decided that such fine buildings could not possibly be the work of Africans. Some experts thought that whites, or an ancient people called the Phoenicians (fuh NIHSH unz), built Great Zimbabwe. Today, we know that an African people called the Shona built Great Zimbabwe about 1,000 years ago.

The Great Enclosure *(far left)* at Great Zimbabwe is more than 23 feet (7 meters) tall. Within and around it are many smaller enclosures that once surrounded huts. The mysterious tower *(near left)* in the Great Enclosure may have been a symbolic storage bin or a symbol of the chief's power.

From the Kid Fact Files

Name: Sacagawea

Home: United States

Birthdate: 1787?

Claim to Fame: Teen-age explorer on the famous Lewis and Clark expedition

Do you like to explore the skies, the oceans, or land? This is the story of a young girl who helped explore the Northwestern United States.

Hello! I'm Sacagawea (sah KAH guh WEE uh). My name means "Bird Woman." I'm a Native American, one of the Shoshone (shoh SHOH nee) people.

I have had many adventures. When I was only a young girl, Minnetaree Indians raided my village. I became a slave. Then my owner lost me in a gambling game. The winner, a French-Canadian trader named Toussaint Charbonneau, made me his wife.

When I was a teen-ager, two American explorers needed our help. They were Meriwether Lewis and William Clark. They wanted to reach the coast of the Pacific Ocean, in a region known as Oregon.

A great wilderness stood between that ocean and our home in what is now North Dakota. The U.S. President

Thomas Jefferson had sent Lewis and Clark to explore the Missouri River and other rivers that would lead to the Pacific Ocean.

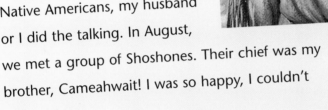

We set off in April 1805. I strapped my new baby, Pomp, to my back.

Whenever we met other Native Americans, my husband or I did the talking. In August, we met a group of Shoshones. Their chief was my brother, Cameahwait! I was so happy, I couldn't stop crying.

But mostly the trip was hard. If we came to rapids or waterfalls, we sometimes had to carry our canoes. A flash flood nearly killed Pomp, Toussaint, and me. We fought grizzlies. We were so hungry we ate our horses.

The last river we followed was the Columbia. Finally, in November, we reached its mouth—at the Pacific Ocean! We had helped the explorers reach their goal.

We spent the winter nearby, at Fort Clatsop. We started our return trip in the spring of 1806. In August, we reached our home, and Lewis and Clark continued on to St. Louis.

My husband was paid $500 for his work. And me? I wasn't paid a penny.

Famous and Fabulous Tombs

Don't be afraid. Walk through the weeping willows, into the Fact Factory's garden of graves. Any mummy would get all wrapped up in these facts.

More than 2 million huge blocks
About 100,000 workers built the Great Pyramid in Giza, Egypt, about 4,500 years ago. King Khufu was buried there. The Great Pyramid has more than 2 million stone blocks. Each block weighs about 2-1/2 tons (2.3 metric tons), which is heavier than seventy 10-year-olds!

Seven giraffes high

A massive tomb (TOOM) was built in what is now Turkey over 2,000 years ago. It was built for the Persian leader Mausolus. Measuring 135 feet (41 meters) high, the tomb was about as tall as seven giraffes standing on top of one another. The building so impressed people that *mausoleum* (MAW suh LEE uhm) became another word for *tomb*.

600 acres—underground!

Don't forget to look underground. Early Christians built catacombs (KAT uh kohmz) in Rome, Italy. They dug out rooms and corridors and cut graves into the walls. These catacombs cover about 600 acres (240 hectares). That's bigger than 450 football fields!

Monk's Mound, in the United States

More than 100 mounds

That enormous hill of dirt is a mass grave.
The hill, known as Monk's Mound, is in what is
now Illinois. Sometime between the 700's and
1700's, the Mississippian people built the hill.
Monk's Mound is bigger at its base than the
Great Pyramid! Workers carried the huge
amounts of soil needed on their backs. More
than 100 other mounds once stood nearby.

One ray of sunshine

Newgrange (nyoo GRAYNJ) is an ancient Irish grave. It has an underground corridor leading to a burial chamber. When the sun rises on the winter solstice, the shortest day of the year, it shines through an opening in the chamber. This lights up carvings on the walls, and the burial chamber glows with an eerie light. Then the sun rises higher, and the burial chamber is wrapped in darkness for another year.

20 years to build

One of the world's most beautiful buildings is a tomb in India called the Taj Mahal (TAHJ muh HAHL). In the 1600's, a ruler called Shah Jahan (SHAH juh HAHN) ordered that the tomb be built of white marble to house the body of his favorite wife, Mumtaz Mahal. It took 20,000 workers about 20 years to finish the job.

Taj Mahal, in India

Which Is Tallest? You Decide!

For 22 years, the tallest building on Earth was Chicago's Sears Tower. Then in 1996, two rival skyscrapers were completed—the Petronas Towers, in Kuala Lumpur, Malaysia.

Alex, from Chicago, thinks Sears Tower is still number one. Lisma, from Kuala Lumpur, disagrees. What do you think?

Alex: Sears Tower has 110 stories. The Petronas Towers have only 88 stories each.

Sears Tower, Chicago

58

Lisma: So? Each of the Petronas towers is 1,483 feet (452 meters) high—higher than 148 Indian elephants stacked on top of one another. Sears Tower is only 1,450 feet (442 meters) high.

Alex: No fair! The Petronas Towers are highest only if you count the pointy spires on top. And if you count the TV antennas on top of the Sears Tower, it's 1,707 feet (520 meters) high.

Lisma: Sorry, spires are part of a building. TV antennas are not.

Alex: Aargh!!!

Petronas Towers,
Kuala Lumpur

59

Art and Air Pollution

Ouch! That raindrop is rubbing my nose off! I'd like to duck into the Fact Factory, where I'd be safe.

These are scary times for marble statues like me. We love the outdoors, but it's killing us. Why? It's killing us because water in the air mixes with pollution, such as gases from cars, factories, and burning wood. The polluted water falls and is called acid (AS ihd) rain. Acid rain eats into marble, limestone, and other substances. Acid rain also kills fish and harms trees.

Some people are trying to save plants, animals, and statues from acid rain. In Athens, Greece, experts moved six

This sculpture is part of a castle in Germany. It was built in 1702. Can you see how acid rain has hurt the sculpture?

Photo taken in 1908

Acid Rain in Action

You can see for yourself how acid rain damages marble statues. Just place a piece of chalk in vinegar for several days. How does the chalk look?

Vinegar is an acid. Chalk is made of calcium carbonate (KAL see uhm KAHR buh nayt), which dissolves in acid. Marble also contains calcium carbonate, so acid rain wears away marble too.

marble statues from an ancient temple called the Erechtheum (er uhk THEE uhm). For thousands of years, these statues held up the roof. Today, they are in a museum, and cement statues hold up the roof instead.

Of course, the best way to protect us is to cut down the air pollution. Then we can all enjoy the outdoors again.

Photo taken in 1998

Make a Miniature Earth

It's a fact that our Earth naturally recycles. It uses the same water and air again and again. Try building a mini-Earth, or terrarium (tuh RAIR ee uhm). It works the same way.

THINGS YOU NEED

a large clear bowl

pebbles

charcoal

potting soil

small plants, such as ferns and ivy

plastic wrap

1 Scatter pebbles on the bottom of the bowl. Add a little charcoal. Top with potting soil.

2 Plant the ferns and ivy in the soil, leaving room for them to grow. Water until the soil is damp but not soggy.

3 Cover the bowl with plastic wrap. Put it in a well-lit place, but out of direct sunlight. If the container fogs up, pull back the plastic wrap until the fog goes away.

Your terrarium will take care of itself. Like on Earth, your plants use the same water and air again and again!

Wild About Weather

Are you ready to be frizzled and frozen, windswept and waterlogged? If so, step into the Fact Factory's weather department. I'm Gus T. Storm, and I think weather is thrilling. You never know what's next!

Wet, wet, wet

Does it rain a lot where you live? Kids on the island of Kauai (kah oo ah ee), in Hawaii, see the most rain. One mountain there gets 460 inches (1,168 centimeters) a year. That is more rain than any other place on Earth.

Meanwhile, every year for 59 years, only 3/100 inch (0.76 millimeter) of rain fell on Arica, Chile. You don't need an umbrella there!

WHY is that?

Some of the world's rainiest places are the warm regions near the equator. The strong heat from the sun there makes lots of water evaporate into the air. As the warm air rises, it cools, and the water falls as rain.

Whooosh!

Sometimes windy weather
makes me hold onto my hat
and run for cover. Tornadoes
are the fiercest winds on Earth—
sometimes faster than 300 miles
(480 kilometers) an hour. The United States
gets more tornadoes than anywhere else. They
happen most often in the middle part of the
country, where cold and warm air collide.

North America

South America

Striking

Speaking of stormy
weather, lightning really
can strike the same place twice,
you know. The southern tip of
Florida is the lightning capital
of the world. Every second,
lightning hits Earth about 100
times. That equals about 500
lightning strikes while you
were reading this sentence.

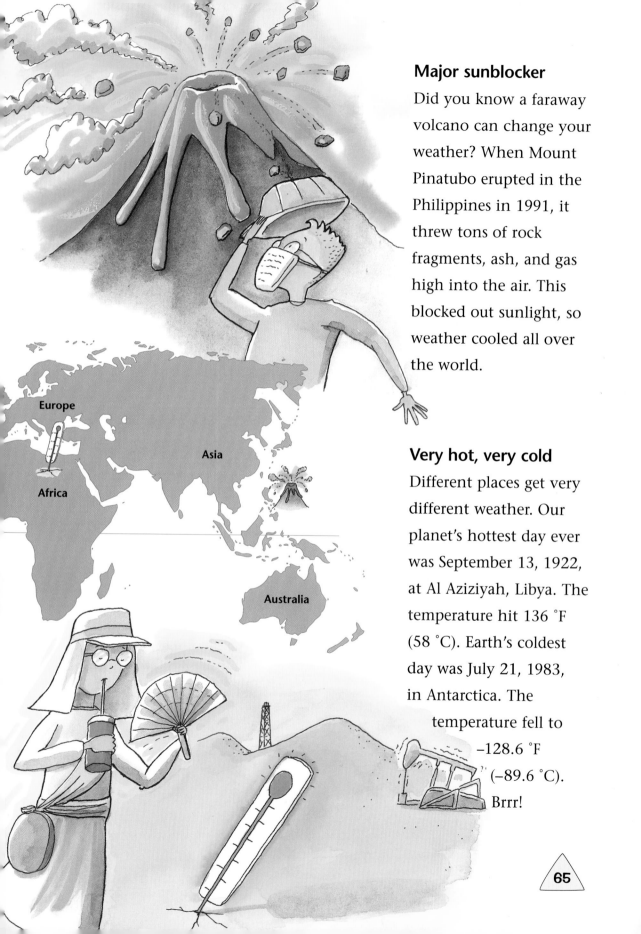

Major sunblocker

Did you know a faraway volcano can change your weather? When Mount Pinatubo erupted in the Philippines in 1991, it threw tons of rock fragments, ash, and gas high into the air. This blocked out sunlight, so weather cooled all over the world.

Europe

Africa

Asia

Australia

Very hot, very cold

Different places get very different weather. Our planet's hottest day ever was September 13, 1922, at Al Aziziyah, Libya. The temperature hit 136 °F (58 °C). Earth's coldest day was July 21, 1983, in Antarctica. The temperature fell to −128.6 °F (−89.6 °C). Brrr!

Faster than the speed of sound

You may have noticed that after a streak of lightning appears, thunder is quick to follow. So why don't we ever hear the thunder first? Thunder and lightning actually happen at the same time. But light travels faster than sound, so we see the lightning first.

Colorful sky

I love rainbows, don't you? If you see a rainbow, that means the sun is behind you, and rain is falling in front of you. Rainbows appear when sunlight passes through raindrops. The raindrops bend the light in such a way that the light breaks up into bands of color. A rainbow's outer band is red, and its inner band is violet. Try looking above a rainbow. Sometimes you will see a second, lighter

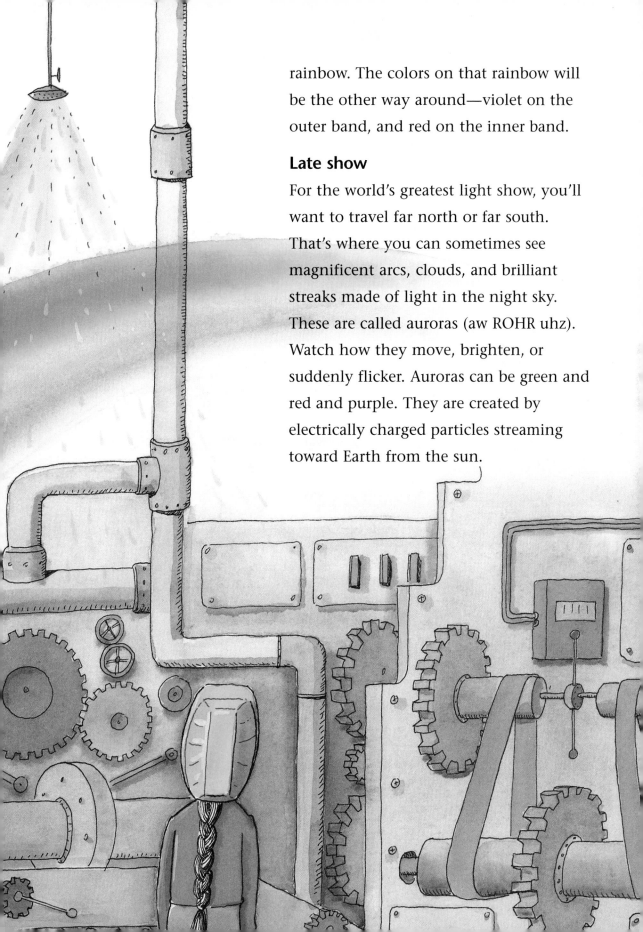

rainbow. The colors on that rainbow will be the other way around—violet on the outer band, and red on the inner band.

Late show

For the world's greatest light show, you'll want to travel far north or far south. That's where you can sometimes see magnificent arcs, clouds, and brilliant streaks made of light in the night sky. These are called auroras (aw ROHR uhz). Watch how they move, brighten, or suddenly flicker. Auroras can be green and red and purple. They are created by electrically charged particles streaming toward Earth from the sun.

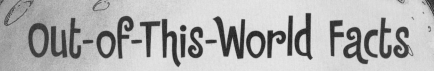

Out-of-This-World Facts

Stella Wilde is my name, selling space is my game! Fact is, the factory's running out of room on Earth. Hop into my craft. I'll show you some available spaces on other planets. First we will head to the planet closest to the sun, Mercury. The sun looks more than twice as big, but the sky is always black. The sky is black because Mercury lacks atmosphere to scatter the light. It is likely you would always see stars there, even during the day!

Mercury

Do you like heat? Or do you prefer cold? Whatever, Mercury is for you. It can get up to 801 °F (427 °C) by day and down to –279 °F (–173 °C) by night. Now that's what I call mercurial!

Our next planet is Venus. Its yellow clouds are lovely, but pure poison. They are made of sulfuric acid (suhl FYOOR ihk AS ihd). Hey, you can't have everything!

Did you ever wish your birthday lasted longer? On Earth, a day lasts 24 hours—that's how long it takes Earth to spin once. On Earth, a year lasts 365 days—that's how long it takes to orbit around the sun. On Venus, a day is longer than a year. A day lasts 243 earth-days, and a year lasts 225 earth-days. Your birthday would be more than a year long, so it would always be your birthday.

We'll just zip past Earth on our way to Mars. Earth is so blue because it is the only planet with oceans.

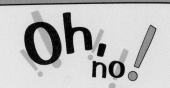

Scientists once thought the planet Venus would be much like Earth, but warmer. They were wrong. Venus is *extremely* hot, and its atmosphere is *very* heavy. The first few space probes that scientists sent to Venus were *squashed* by its atmosphere before they could send back information!

Mars looks a lot like Earth, except for being so red, of course. Most of Mars is reddish desertlike regions of dust, sand, and rocks. The deep canyons in the land look like dried-up riverbeds. Some scientists think there was life on Mars billions of years ago.

Mars also has the biggest known volcano in our solar system. It is more than twice as high as Earth's Mount Everest!

Jupiter

The Fact Factory needs lots of room for new facts, so Jupiter is ideal. It's our largest planet— bigger than 1,000 Earths. In fact, Jupiter's Great Red Spot alone, an everlasting storm of swirling gas, is bigger than our Earth! The only thing missing on Jupiter is land.

Jupiter's surface is made of thick red, brown, yellow, and white clouds of gas. And time really flies here. Jupiter has the shortest day in the solar system. It's less than 10 hours long!

Let's check out the next planet, Saturn. It is a ball of liquids and gases. Just look at those glittering rings spinning around it. They are made of billions of bits of ice. And if you like moons, Saturn has at least 18!

Saturn

Oh, no!

English-speaking scientists once thought Mars had canals dug by Martians. An Italian scientist had observed lines on Mars. He called them *canali* in Italian, which means "channels" in English. But people thought the word meant "canals" in English. Of course, Mars has no canals, and no Martians either, as far as we know!

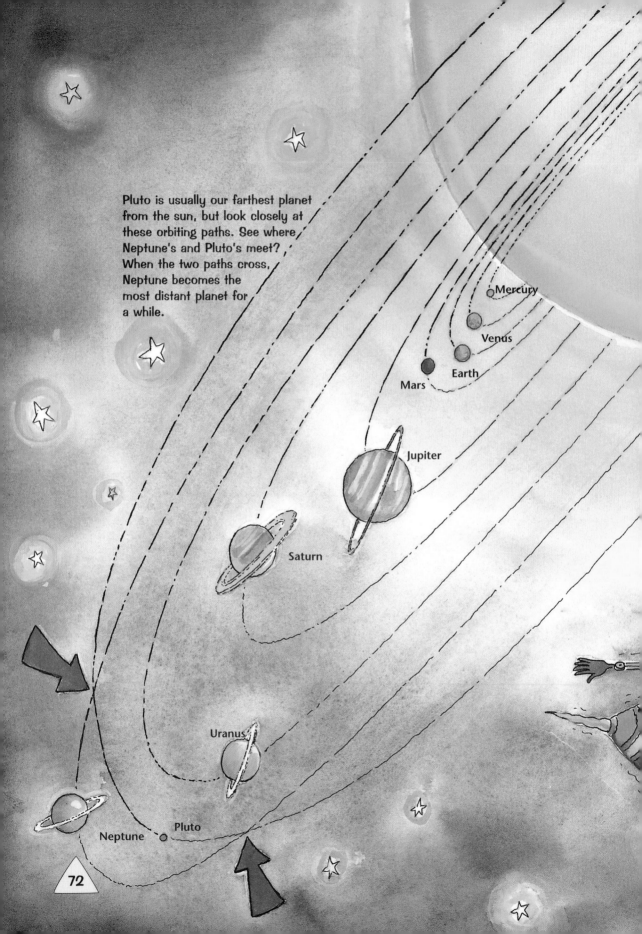

Pluto is usually our farthest planet from the sun, but look closely at these orbiting paths. See where Neptune's and Pluto's meet? When the two paths cross, Neptune becomes the most distant planet for a while.

Mercury

Venus

Earth

Mars

Jupiter

Saturn

Uranus

Neptune   Pluto

WHY is that?

Who is older, an 8-year-old person on Earth or an 8-year-old on Pluto? An 8-year-old on Pluto. That's because a year on Pluto lasts about 248 earth-years. An 8-year-old there would be 8 x 248, or 1,984 earth-years old!

Suppose you grew up on Pluto. How old would you be in earth-years?

Next on our list is Uranus (YUR uh nuhs). Whee! This planet really tilts. It looks like it's rolling along on its side!

Bright blue-green clouds of gas make up Uranus's surface. Near the south pole, fierce winds make these clouds spin faster than the rest of Uranus. So, a day near the south pole is only 14 hours long, but a day lasts 17 hours on the rest of the planet!

Here comes Neptune! Sorry if things get a bit bumpy. Neptune is a windy planet. Neptune's clouds whip around the planet at speeds up to 700 miles (1,125 kilometers) per hour.

Neptune is usually the eighth planet from the sun. But every 248 years, Neptune moves farther from the sun and Pluto moves closer. Then Neptune becomes the most distant planet for a while.

Let's just take a quick peek at Pluto. It's the smallest planet—less than one-fifth as wide as Earth. Scientists think Pluto is very icy, but nobody knows for sure.

Which planet would you prefer to call home?

Factory Fun

It's A-maze-ing What You Know!

Which of the following facts are true? Which facts are false? Choose the right answers to make your way from one side of Earth to the other. Choose the wrong answers, and you may end up back where you started.

9 Coral is made of skeletons.

10 Lightning can strike the same place twice.

7 Asia is the biggest and most crowded continent.

8 Ancient Troy was a real place.

6 Air pollution is damaging structures that are thousands of years old.

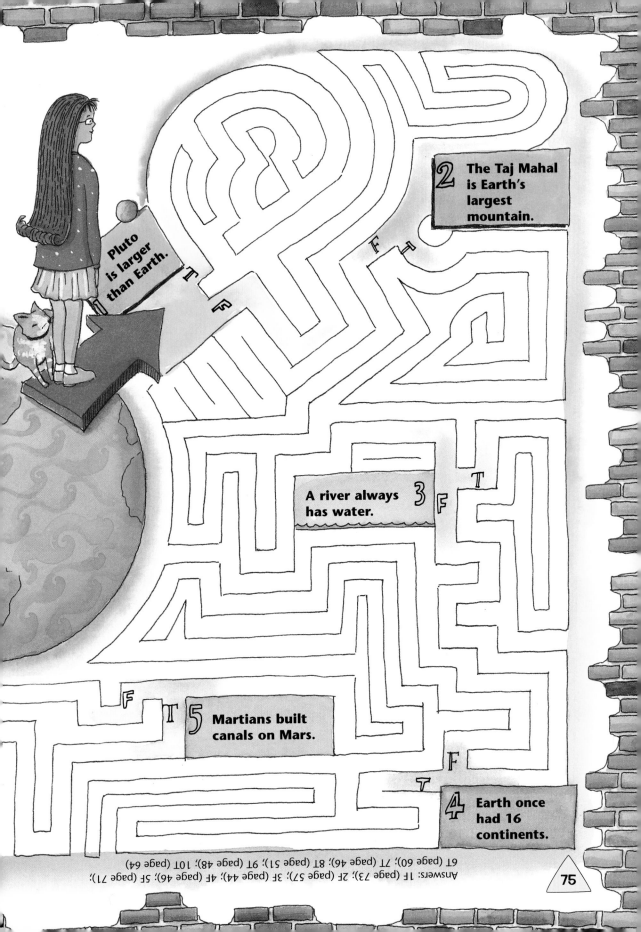

Pluto is larger than Earth.

1. T F

2. The Taj Mahal is Earth's largest mountain. T F

3. A river always has water. F T

4. Earth once had 16 continents. T F

5. Martians built canals on Mars. F T

Answers: 1F (page 73); 2F (page 57); 3F (page 44); 4F (page 46); 5F (page 71); 6T (page 60); 7T (page 46); 8T (page 51); 9T (page 48); 10T (page 64)

75

People Facts

The factory is full of all kinds of people, just as there are all kinds of people on Earth. If you could sit and watch people for hours, you would see that they are amazing specimens. They have different kinds of families, different ways of doing things, and lots of different ideas. Look at the following pages, and you may even learn a few things about yourself!

Many Kinds of Families

Hi, I'm Lotta Frendz, head of the factory's People Facts. You already know a family can be very small, such as one parent and one child. It can also be very large and include parents, children, grandparents, aunts, uncles, and cousins. But did you know the following family facts?

If you live in a San (san) family in Africa, your family has about 25 people. Actually, it includes several families. In a Hopi (HOH pee) family in the southwestern United States, the oldest woman is regarded as the head of the family. In many parts of India, your uncle and his wife and children live with your family.

In a Masai (mah SY) family in Kenya, a boy does not plan to marry until he is about 30. After childhood, he must first become a junior warrior and then a senior warrior. Then he may marry, become

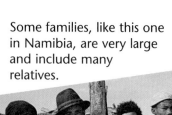

Some families, like this one in Namibia, are very large and include many relatives.

a junior elder, and then become a senior elder. A girl can marry in her teens.

How many brothers and sisters do you have? If you live in the United States, chances are that you have fewer brothers and sisters than your

Some families, like this one in Russia, are small.

grandparents or great-grandparents did. In 1900, more than five children were born in the average family. Today there are about two.

Who is in your family?

In 1900, a typical family in the United States had more than five children. Today, most families have about two.

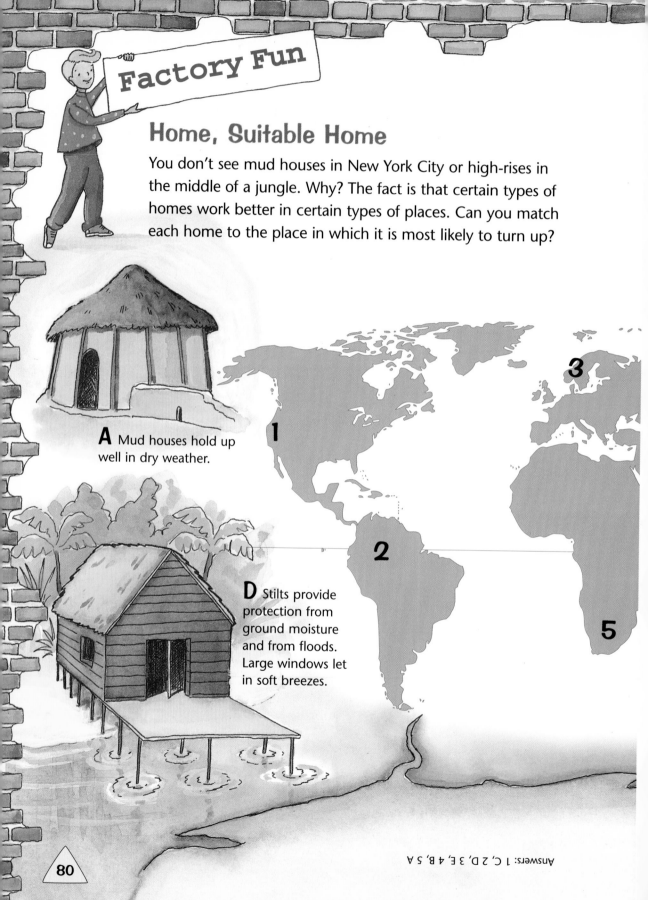

Factory Fun

Home, Suitable Home

You don't see mud houses in New York City or high-rises in the middle of a jungle. Why? The fact is that certain types of homes work better in certain types of places. Can you match each home to the place in which it is most likely to turn up?

A Mud houses hold up well in dry weather.

D Stilts provide protection from ground moisture and from floods. Large windows let in soft breezes.

Answers: 1 C, 2 D, 3 E, 4 B, 5 A

1 San Francisco is a crowded city also known for its earthquakes.

2 Villages in the Amazon Rain Forest have hot, humid, rainy weather all year.

3 Norway is a snowy place. About 3 1/2 feet (1 meter) of snow falls in some parts each year.

4 In China, the housing shortage is so great that people live on small boats in rivers and harbors.

5 The plains of Botswana receive little rain. Parts are even desertlike.

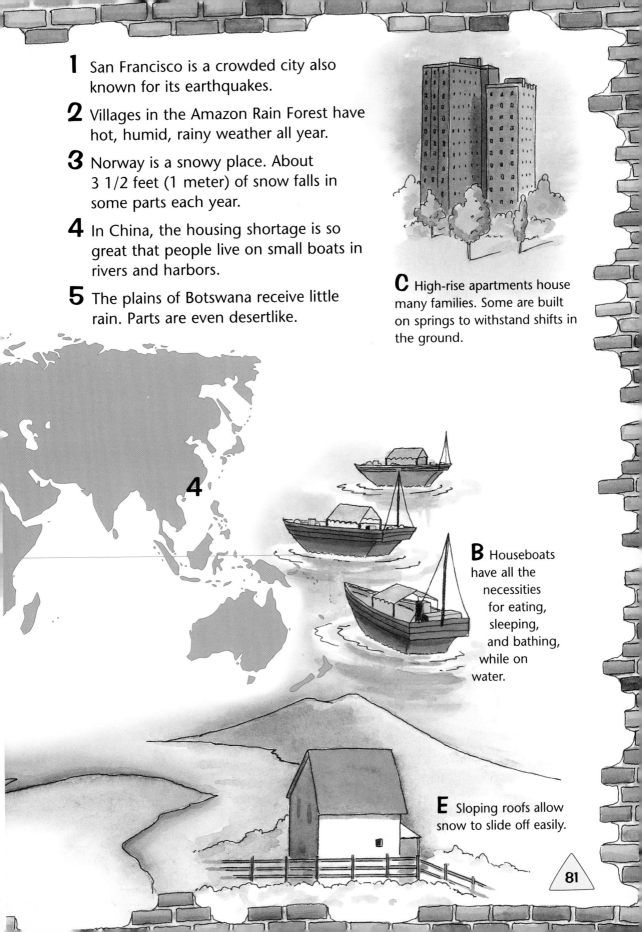

C High-rise apartments house many families. Some are built on springs to withstand shifts in the ground.

B Houseboats have all the necessities for eating, sleeping, and bathing, while on water.

E Sloping roofs allow snow to slide off easily.

Where Is Everybody?

One, two, three . . . We do lots of counting around here. We're keeping an eye on people around the world.

How are people counted?

Did you know that most countries take a census (SEHN suhs)? A census is a count of their people. The census is used to find out such things as where the people live, how many are males, how many are females, their ages, and what language they speak. Most countries also keep records that show how many people are born each year and how many people die. Let me show you some more facts that are gathered from a census.

There are lots of us!

How many people do you think live on Earth? If you said nearly 6 billion, you would

These people represent the population of the world 150 years ago . . .

WHY is that?

One whole continent has no countries and no permanent people. Scientists visit it, but nobody lives there year round. It's Antarctica, at the South Pole. Antarctica is too cold for most people to live and work.

be correct. That's nearly five times as many as there were 150 years ago.

Our numbers are growing fast! Right now, the world gets more than 100 million new people per year. That's enough to fill six cities the size of New York City.

. . . and these people represent the world population today.

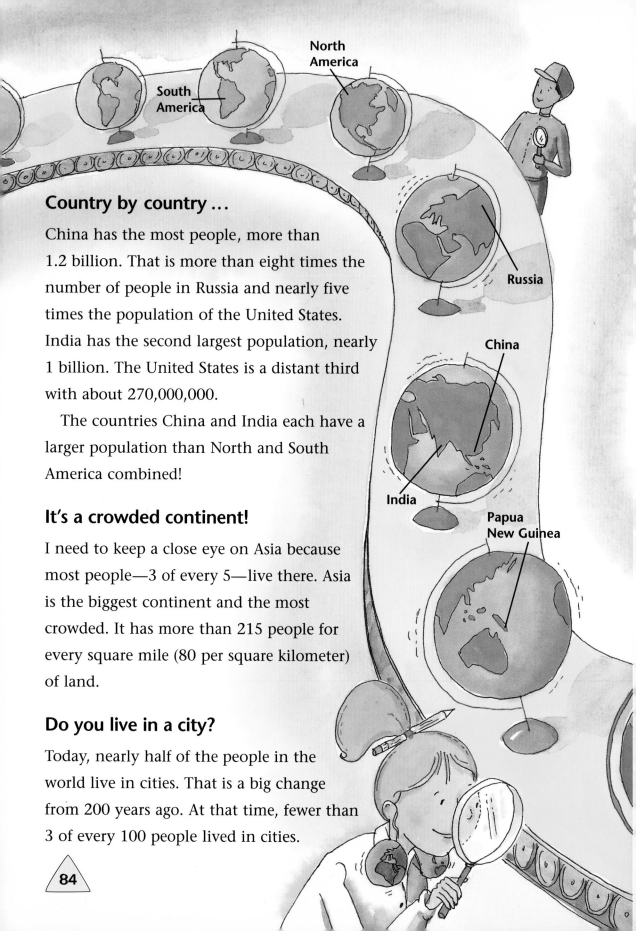

South
America

North
America

Russia

China

India

Papua
New Guinea

Country by country...

China has the most people, more than
1.2 billion. That is more than eight times the
number of people in Russia and nearly five
times the population of the United States.
India has the second largest population, nearly
1 billion. The United States is a distant third
with about 270,000,000.

The countries China and India each have a
larger population than North and South
America combined!

It's a crowded continent!

I need to keep a close eye on Asia because
most people—3 of every 5—live there. Asia
is the biggest continent and the most
crowded. It has more than 215 people for
every square mile (80 per square kilometer)
of land.

Do you live in a city?

Today, nearly half of the people in the
world live in cities. That is a big change
from 200 years ago. At that time, fewer than
3 of every 100 people lived in cities.

Pardon me?

What language is spoken by the most people? English? Guess again! It's Mandarin Chinese. The runners-up, in order, are English, Hindi, and Spanish.

To hear the most languages spoken, go to Papua New Guinea. That country has more than 850 languages. Each is spoken by about 4,000 people.

tet
tot
vot

Living longer

In the United States, people born in 1900 lived an average of about 47 years. People born today can expect to live nearly thirty years longer!

Asia

Life spans

Are you keeping count of all these numbers and people? Do you know where people are living longest? People are living longest in Japan. In that country, on average, a person lives to be 80 years old. People in China average 79 years.

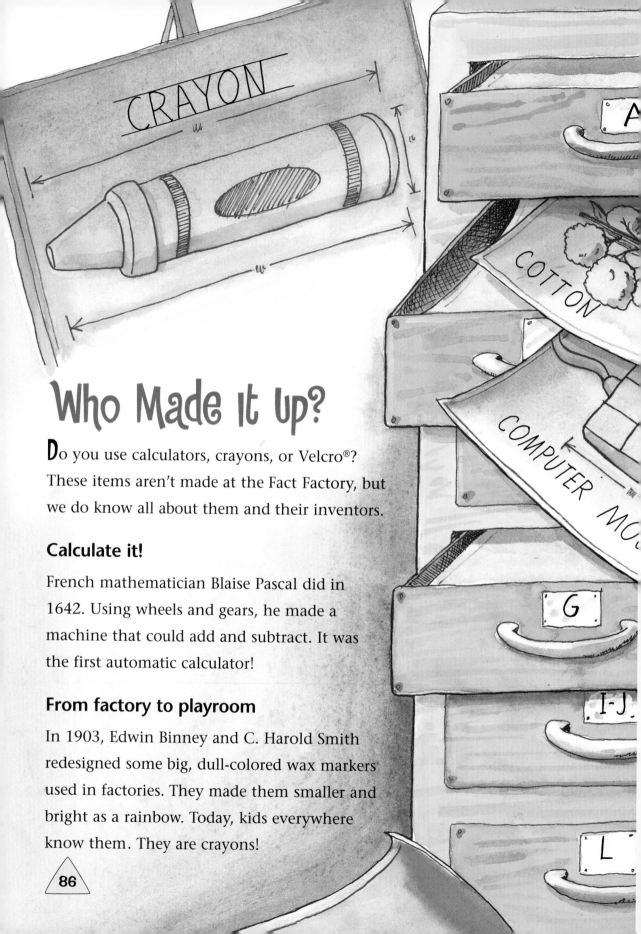

CRAYON

Who Made it Up?

Do you use calculators, crayons, or Velcro®? These items aren't made at the Fact Factory, but we do know all about them and their inventors.

Calculate it!

French mathematician Blaise Pascal did in 1642. Using wheels and gears, he made a machine that could add and subtract. It was the first automatic calculator!

From factory to playroom

In 1903, Edwin Binney and C. Harold Smith redesigned some big, dull-colored wax markers used in factories. They made them smaller and bright as a rainbow. Today, kids everywhere know them. They are crayons!

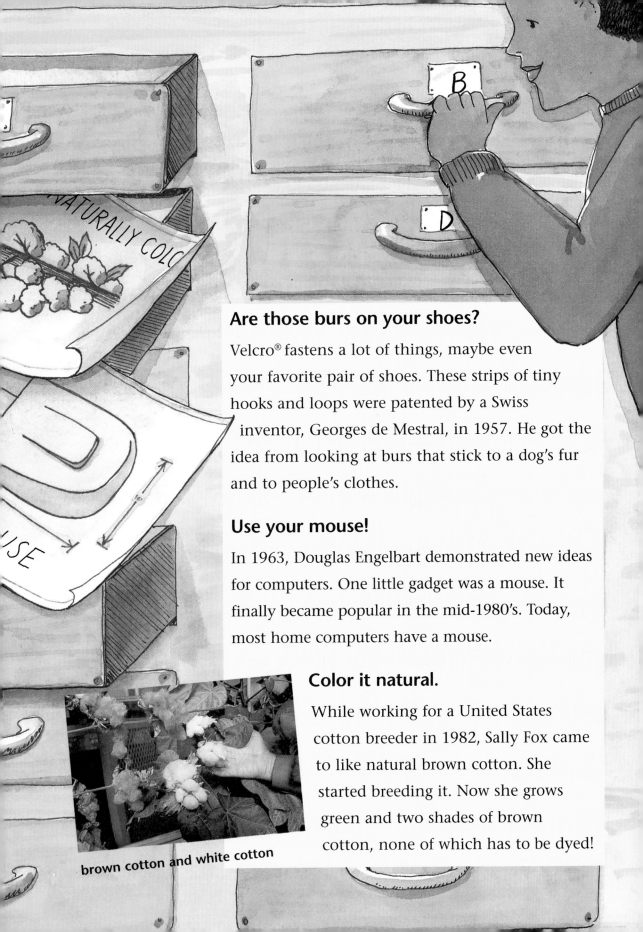

Are those burs on your shoes?

Velcro® fastens a lot of things, maybe even your favorite pair of shoes. These strips of tiny hooks and loops were patented by a Swiss inventor, Georges de Mestral, in 1957. He got the idea from looking at burs that stick to a dog's fur and to people's clothes.

Use your mouse!

In 1963, Douglas Engelbart demonstrated new ideas for computers. One little gadget was a mouse. It finally became popular in the mid-1980's. Today, most home computers have a mouse.

Color it natural.

While working for a United States cotton breeder in 1982, Sally Fox came to like natural brown cotton. She started breeding it. Now she grows green and two shades of brown cotton, none of which has to be dyed!

brown cotton and white cotton

Who Got There First?

People not only invent helpful gadgets, but they also find new ways to get where they are going. Here are some fabulous "firsts" in travel.

Moving up in the world

Two French papermakers, the Montgolfier brothers, launched the first balloon in June 1783. Five months later, their first passenger balloon carried a scientist and a nobleman aloft for 25 minutes.

I'll be back . . . next week!

Wiley Post, a U.S. pilot, made the first solo around-the-world trip in 1933. It took him almost eight days.

Wiley Post

Chuck
Yeager

Breaking the
sound barrier

United States Air Force pilot
Chuck (Charles E.) Yeager
was the first person to fly
faster than the speed of
sound. He did it October 14,
1947, flying a rocket airplane.

Cruising around Earth

Soviet cosmonaut Yuri Gagarin became the first human in space when he orbited Earth once on April 12, 1961. The trip took 108 minutes. Cosmonaut Valentina Tereshkova became the first woman in space on June 16, 1963. She orbited Earth for almost three days.

Cosmonaut Valentina Tereshkova was the first woman in space.

Can you imagine how it felt to be the first person to walk on the moon?

Walking on the moon

United States astronauts Neil Armstrong, "Buzz" (Edwin) Aldrin, and Michael Collins made the first moon landing. Their flight blasted off July 16, 1969. Armstrong and Aldrin landed and walked on the moon on July 20.

From the Kid Fact Files

Name: Louis Braille

Birthdate: January 4, 1809

Hometown: Coupvray, France

Claim to Fame: Invented a writing and printing system for the blind

From the files comes this story about a boy who became a famous young inventor. His work has helped many people to read and write and communicate.

I lived in Paris for several years, while my family lived in the little town of Coupvray, not far away.

My father had his own leather shop. When I was a small child, I loved to play there. One day, when I was 3, I grabbed one of the sharp tools. I injured one eye with it, and both eyes became infected. That's how I became blind.

My parents thought I could learn. When the village priest came to see my parents, he thought so, too. At first he taught me by reading to me and telling me about things. But I wanted so much to go to school! He persuaded the schoolmaster to let me try, and I went to school with the other children my age. Learning was easy, because I could remember everything I heard. But I couldn't read or write.

When I was 10, I got a scholarship to a school for the blind in Paris. A few good students were allowed to learn to read special books. Finally I learned to read by feeling large, raised letters with my fingers. But tracing the letters took so long! And there were only a few of the special books. I was a good musician, too. I learned to play the piano and organ by touch. I thought reading should be at least as easy as that!

Braille Code

A braille book has words printed as a series of raised dots. Blind people read by running their fingertips over the dots. The braille cell is three dots high and two dots wide.

The braille alphabet starts by using 10 combinations of the top 4 dots.

A   B   C   D   E   F   G   H   I   J

Adding the lower left-hand dot makes the next 10 letters.

K   L   M   N   O   P   Q   R   S   T

Adding the lower right-hand dot makes the last five letters of the alphabet (except w) and five word symbols.

U   V   X   Y   Z   and   for   of   the   with

Taking away the lower left-hand dot forms the following sounds and the letter w.

ch   gh   sh   th   wh   ed   er   ou   ow   W

When I was about 12, an army captain, Charles Barbier de la Serre, came to our school. He had invented a code of twelve raised dots called "night writing" that soldiers could read in the dark. But the army had turned it down. The code used dots and dashes instead of large, raised letters. Each arrangement of dots and dashes stood for a sound. Some of us were allowed to try it.

We could read this code. But I thought it could be simpler, and I decided to work on it.

From that time on, I spent every spare moment on the code. By the time I was 15, I had figured out a six-dot system. Each arrangement of dots stood for a letter, so words could be spelled the same way as in print. And the dots could easily be punched into paper. I could use them to write!

When I was 18, I transcribed the first book for the blind. Later, I became a teacher in the school, and I invented a way to write music for the blind, too.

What Is Your Body Saying?

In my job, I make friends in many countries. But I learned that I have to pay attention to what I say, not only with words, but with my face, hands, and even my feet.

Do you nod "yes" and shake your head "no"? People in Bulgaria and Sri Lanka do just the opposite.

Tapping the side of your forehead can mean "really smart" in the United States. In the Netherlands, tapping the middle of the forehead means "crazy."

In the United States, people whistle to cheer a favorite team or singer. But in Europe, whistling means "No good!"

Have you ever received a pat on the head for a job well done? You wouldn't in most parts of Asia. There it is not appropriate to touch a person's head.

In Spain, talking with your hands in your pockets is rude.

Is it polite to stick out your tongue? In Tibet it is a form of greeting.

Do you point to objects with your finger? In Thailand, a person points with the chin, not a hand.

Have you ever motioned with your finger for someone to come to you? In China, that is rude. There and in other countries, people motion to each other with their palm down and by bending and moving their fingers back and forth.

In many countries, making a circle with your pointer finger and thumb says, "It's okay." But

WHY is that?

When people began shaking hands, it was not just to say hello. It was also a way to show they weren't carrying weapons and wouldn't start a fight!

in France, it can also mean "It's worthless." In Japan, it stands for money. And in Greece and Italy it can be an insult!

"Feet on the floor" is the safest way to sit. In many Arab countries, it is bad manners to show the sole of your shoe.

One kind of body language is a friendly gesture everywhere. It's a smile.

How Well Do You Know Your Body?

At the Fact Factory, there are thousands of facts about the human body. Just take a look at this prize-winning information!

Your largest organ

What do you think is your largest organ? Your lungs? Your stomach? No, It's your skin! A person who weighs 100 pounds (45 kilograms) has about 10 pounds (4.5 kilograms) of skin.

Being flaky

Dandruff is not a disease you can catch. Everyone's skin has a tough, dead outer layer that flakes off. People with dandruff just have patches that flake off faster.

Twitches in your muscles

Muscles make your body move. They contain slow-twitch fibers and fast-twitch fibers. Different people have different amounts of each. People with more fast-twitch fibers in their legs are more likely to be good sprinters. People with more slow-twitch fibers are more likely to be good distance runners.

How strong is your face?

Some of the strongest muscles you have are in your face! They are the muscles you use when you chew.

When you swallow food, it does not just fall into your stomach. Rippling muscles push it along. So you could swallow even if you were traveling in space, away from the earth's gravity.

Thank your liver

When your body uses food, it makes a lot of ammonia, a harmful chemical. But you don't need to worry. Your liver gets rid of it by changing it into a harmless chemical.

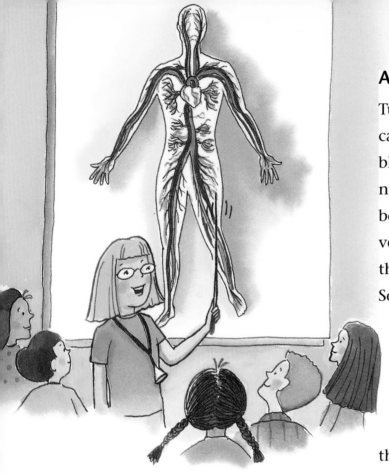

A really tight squeeze

Tubes called arteries carry your blood. Your blood carries oxygen and nutrients to your outer body parts. The tiniest vessels your blood goes through are capillaries. Some of them are even narrower than your red blood cells. But your heart pumps so strongly that it pushes the blood cells through them.

Painful peppers

Ouch! If you touch something sharp or hot, you quickly jerk your body back. That's a reflex, an automatic action. Your brain controls your senses. But with reflexes, your spinal cord signals your nerves to move even before the message reaches your brain.

Your tongue has taste buds that can detect sweet, sour, salty, and bitter tastes. But hot chili peppers do not get your taste buds excited. Instead, they send pain messages through nerves in your tongue.

Splash

Do you gasp when cold water hits you? That is because your nerves send "cold" messages to several parts of your brain. One of those parts controls breathing, so you take a big breath when you are splashed!

Happy feet

Your foot has three arches—a large arch from the ball of your foot to the heel, another arch along the outside of your foot, and a smaller arch across the middle of your foot. The arches keep your feet springy and make walking smoother.

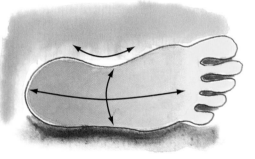

WHY is that?

Do feather pillows make you sneeze? It is probably because you're allergic to tiny bugs called house mites. They live on grains of dust that get in the feathers.

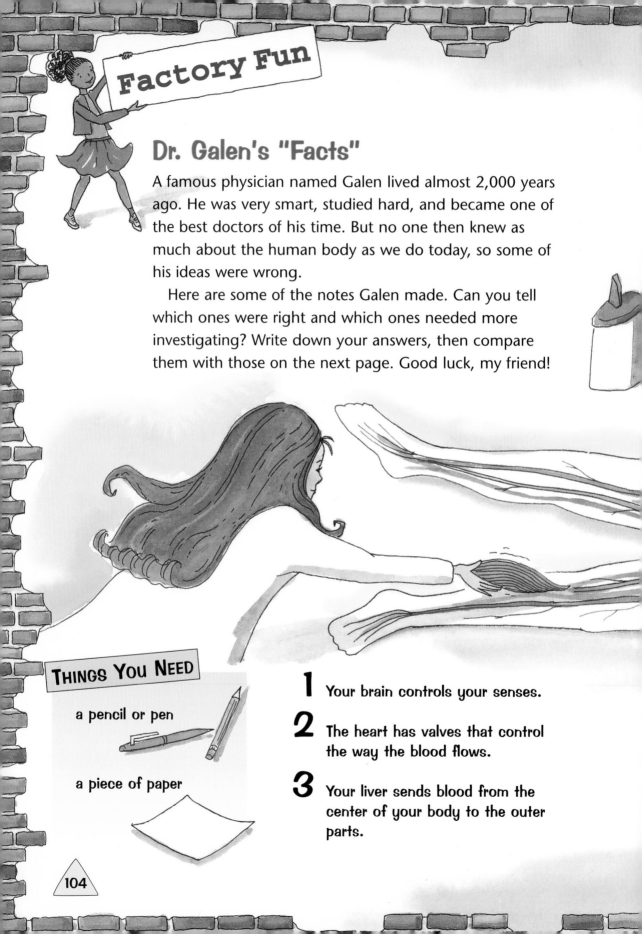

Factory Fun

Dr. Galen's "Facts"

A famous physician named Galen lived almost 2,000 years ago. He was very smart, studied hard, and became one of the best doctors of his time. But no one then knew as much about the human body as we do today, so some of his ideas were wrong.

Here are some of the notes Galen made. Can you tell which ones were right and which ones needed more investigating? Write down your answers, then compare them with those on the next page. Good luck, my friend!

THINGS YOU NEED

a pencil or pen

a piece of paper

1 Your brain controls your senses.

2 The heart has valves that control the way the blood flows.

3 Your liver sends blood from the center of your body to the outer parts.

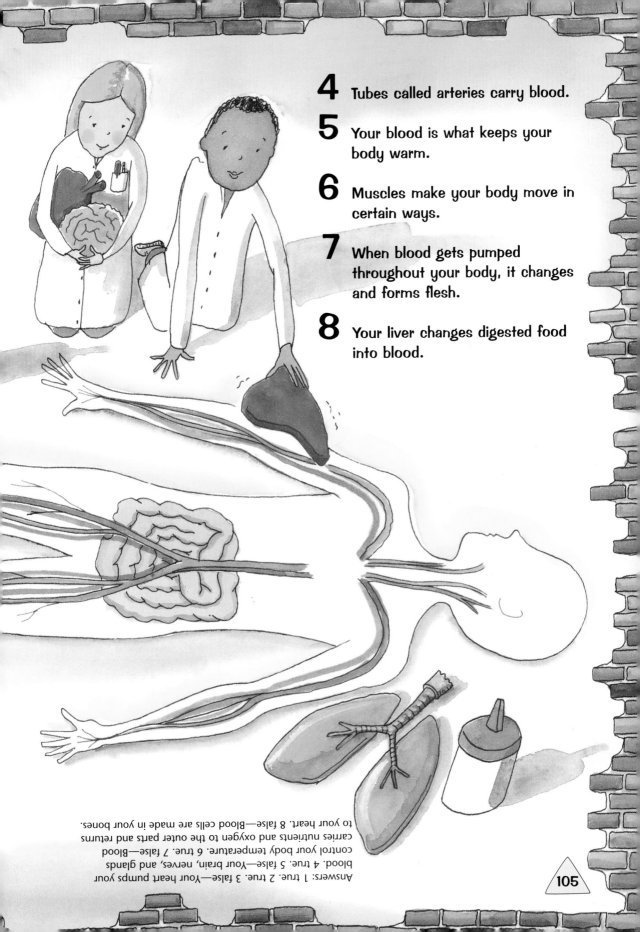

4 Tubes called arteries carry blood.

5 Your blood is what keeps your body warm.

6 Muscles make your body move in certain ways.

7 When blood gets pumped throughout your body, it changes and forms flesh.

8 Your liver changes digested food into blood.

Answers: 1 true. 2 true. 3 false—Your heart pumps your blood. 4 true. 5 false—Your brain, nerves, and glands control your body temperature. 6 true. 7 false—Blood carries nutrients and oxygen to the outer parts and returns to your heart. 8 false—Blood cells are made in your bones.

Footprints in Time

Imagine finding an ancient set of footprints, perfectly preserved. Who could have made them? What facts might the prints have led you to discover? Here's one story.

When the far-off mountain exploded, a little ash fell on us. But we stayed where we were, because the plants were still green and there was enough food.

But then the dry season came. My father kept looking at the sky. My mother began saving food, including seeds and dried plants. That meant we were going to move.

We walked for about five suns. The air was so hot! We could taste ashes in the wind. Then we saw it, a place where heavy ashes had fallen.

The ashes were like a river. We had to cross them. My father's footprints were big

and far apart. My mother's were much smaller. Just for fun, she tried to step in his footprints. Later, I looked back. There were our footprints, showing the way we had come. Maybe you'll see them someday. Or maybe someone else will find them.

In 1978, scientists were working with archaeologist Mary Leakey in Laetoli, Tanzania. In rock formed by volcanic ash, they found fossil footprints of three hominids (HAH muh nihdz), humanlike creatures. The footprints were 3.6 million years old.

Mary Leakey and footprints

Extreme Facts

This world is full of amazing things—the very biggest and the very smallest, the most and the least, the speediest and the slowest, the most dangerous and the most endangered. That is the long and short of it. There are fun facts galore, so let's explore.

smallest

BIGG

LONGEST

Stupendous Facts

In this part of the Fact Factory, we turn out strange facts—the more unusual, the better. Everything in our Stupendous (stoo PEHN duhs) department is simply the most!

People are smart, but sperm whales are "brainier." They have the largest brain of any animal. It weighs up to 20 pounds (9 kilograms).

Horses and ostriches have the largest eyes of all land animals. One of their eyeballs is about the size of a baseball. And an ostrich's eye is larger than its brain! The eye of the giant squid can be 15 inches (40 centimeters) across.

If you ever think the world is full of creepy, crawly things, you are

Oh, no!

The most endangered kinds of living things in the world today are plants. Certain mammals, birds, and fish, are the next most endangered kinds of living things.

right! Scientists have counted more than 1 1/2 million kinds, or species, of animals. About a million of those species are insects.

If you are looking for big insects, say hello to the giant Hercules moth. It has the largest wingspread, up to about 14 inches (35 centimeters) across.

The world's biggest flower is easy to spot, and smell. It is the giant rafflesia (ra FLEE zhuh). It has no stem or leaves, but its blossom can be 3 feet (90 centimeters) across. Don't plant it in your garden though. It smells like rotting meat!

Do you collect leaves? Try for the world's biggest, the raffia (RAF ee uh) palm. It has leaves up to 65 feet (20 meters) long.

Would you like one of the world's tallest dogs? Try an Irish wolfhound or a Great Dane. Both breeds stand up to 39 inches (100 centimeters) tall at the shoulder. That's a little taller than a yardstick, and maybe about as tall as you are.

The Star of Africa is the largest cut diamond in the world. It is a dazzling 530 carats, slightly smaller and heavier than a tennis ball. This diamond is one of the British Crown Jewels.

How about playing the world's biggest guitar? It is 16 feet (4.8 meters) wide, more than 38 feet (11 meters) tall, and weighs 1,865 pounds (846 kilograms). It was made by high school students in Jasonville, Indiana.

The largest asteroid ever known to strike the earth fell near the Yucatán Peninsula, Mexico, about 65 million years ago. It created the Chicxulub Basin, a crater about 190 miles (305 kilometers) wide. Scientists think its collision may have caused weather changes that killed off the dinosaurs!

Want to see the longest fence in the world? It's in Australia and is about 3,300 miles (5,530 kilometers) long. It was built to protect farmers' sheep from wild dogs called dingoes. The Great Wall of China is even longer. It is about 4,000 miles (6,400 kilometers) long and is the longest structure ever built. It was built hundreds of years ago to keep out invaders.

Either one—the fence or the wall—could easily stretch across the entire United States, and farther! The United States is a mere 2,807 miles (4,517 kilometers) across.

Speaking of the United States, almost the entire country could be covered by the Sahara—the world's largest desert.

The world's largest guitar is sure to produce big hits.

Faster than the wind and sound, the
Thrust SSC car has the power of 1,000
Ford Escorts, or 145 Formula One cars.

Are you starting to think big?
Just imagine a vacation on the
world's biggest cruise ship, 951 feet
(290 meters) long, and taller than
the Statue of Liberty. The British
ship *Grand Princess* carries 2,600
passengers and has more than
1,000 crew members. It has five
swimming pools, a small golf
course, and a virtual reality center
for computer-age 3-D adventures.

The world's largest ship takes no
passengers. It is the *Seawise Giant*, a

WHY is that?

The fastest ships are hovercraft and hydrofoils. They travel much faster than even the biggest ships, up to 80 miles (130 kilometers) per hour. That's because they float above the water. Hovercrafts float on a cushion of air made by high-speed fans. A hydrofoil (*below*) skims across the surface on wings attached to its hull.

big tanker. It measures 1,504 feet (458 meters) long, or about three city blocks.

Do you dream about driving the fastest car in the world? The *Thrust SSC,* a supersonic jet car built in Great Britain, set a speed record of more than 763 miles (1,227 kilometers) per hour on a course in the Nevada desert. It also was the first car to exceed the speed of sound!

You will find the longest stairway near Spiez, Switzerland. It rises nearly 5,500 feet (1,677 meters), with 11,674 steps. It is used by service crews on a steep railway.

In Canada, you can cross the longest bridge over water that freezes. The Confederation Bridge links Prince Edward Island with the mainland. It spans nearly 8 miles (13 kilometers) and takes 10 minutes to drive across.

Care to climb the stairs to the tops of three of the largest skyscrapers? That's how far you would have to walk to climb the world's longest stairway, in Switzerland!

Find the most!

Make your own collection of the biggest, tallest, longest, fastest, or most things in your city or town. Can you find the tallest building? How about the oldest house or store or school? What is the longest street? What is the coldest or the hottest weather anyone can remember? Share your list of stupendous facts with your family and friends.

Akashi Kaikyo bridge, Japan

You will have to travel to Japan to cross the world's longest suspension bridge. The Akashi Kaikyo bridge was completed in 1998. It has a main span of 6,529 feet (1,990 meters), or about 12 city blocks. It connects the city of Kobe with Awaji Island.

If you are up for traveling, how about touring the world's largest country? It's Russia! It covers more than 6 million square miles (17 million square kilometers) of land. That is almost twice the size of the United States.

From the Kid Fact Files

Name: Albert Einstein

Home: Munich, Germany

Birthdate: March 14, 1879

Claim to Fame: Discovered relativity and was one of the greatest scientists of all time

Everyone at the factory adores extreme thinkers. Don't you? Just imagine what it would have been like to be Albert Einstein, who was born in 1879 in Germany . . .

When I was a child in Munich, Germany, my mother was worried about me. I was a big, quiet, unusual-looking baby, and I didn't talk until I was 3 years old. But I was curious about things. When I was about five, my father showed me his compass. What a mysterious thing it was! I wondered what made the needle always point north. And my mother taught me to be independent. By the time I was 4, I was learning to find my way around the busy city streets by myself.

At first I was taught at home. When I was 7, I was sent to school. My teachers and classmates did not think I had much talent because I didn't answer quickly enough, especially in arithmetic. In my next school, I thought the classes were boring! But my uncle taught me algebra at home. Algebra (AL juh bruh) is a kind of mathematics that

uses symbols and letters that stand for unknown numbers. For example:

$$2x + 3x = 5x$$

Working with unknown numbers was fun. I taught myself geometry from a book. Geometry (jee AHM uh tree) is a kind of mathematics that deals with lines, angles, and shapes, such as:

One of my parents' friends gave me some wonderful science books. Whenever he came to dinner, we talked about the ideas in those books.

In college, I learned mathematics and science easily. The ideas were exciting! But if I didn't like a class, I skipped it. I skipped so many classes that several professors told me I would not graduate. But a friend lent me his notes. I studied hard, passed my exams, and got my degree after all. My next step was to find work. Some of my professors were annoyed with me. They wouldn't help. I wrote a paper that was published in an important science magazine, but that didn't help, either. In 1902, after several temporary jobs, I finally went to work in the Swiss patent office.

My work in the patent office left me with plenty of time to think. I began to think about the motions of particles, the nature of light, and the passage of time. In one year, 1905, I wrote five papers about three important ideas. One of those ideas became a popular theory of relativity, which is still very important in science today.

My ideas did not agree with the thinking of other scientists at the time. But some scientists were interested in them. Soon I got teaching jobs in Zurich and Prague. Then I was offered a director's job at a university in Berlin. Years after my first papers were published, scientists used an eclipse of the sun to do an experiment with light. The results were exactly what my theory predicted. Suddenly I was famous! In 1921, I won the Nobel Prize in physics.

Minuscule Facts

Watch your head, friend. The ceilings in this tiny room are low! Here is where we handle minuscule (MIHN uhs kyool) facts. *Minuscule* is a great big word, but it means "very small." So these facts are about the smallest, slowest, least, or fewest things in the world.

One of the smallest insects is the tiny fairy fly. We can hardly see it, but it can fly through the eye of a needle.

The smallest bird is the bee hummingbird. It is about 2 inches (5 centimeters) long and weighs about 1/10 ounce (3 grams). It builds a nest that is the size of half a walnut shell.

The smallest plant with fruit and flowers is a duckweed that grows in Australia. This water plant is only about 2/100 inch (0.05 cm) long. Its fruit looks like a tiny fig. It is minuscule!

The smallest mammal is Kitti's hognose bat. It lives in Thailand. It is about the size of a bumblebee, and it weighs about as much as a U.S. penny.

If you want to see an animal in slow motion, watch for a sloth. The slowest-moving, least active mammal is the three-toed tree sloth. And you can't say its name fast either!

This illustration shows the bee hummingbird, at its actual size!

Least is more!

The least-endangered living things are conifers (KOH nuh fuhrs), cone-bearing trees. Only four species are endangered or threatened. Conifers also include the largest, tallest, and oldest living things.

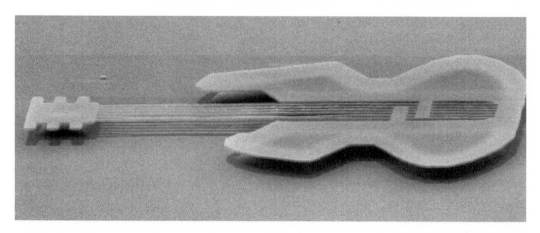

Don't try to strum this guitar—you'd squash it, if you could find it! The nanoguitar looks life-size in this photo, but in fact it is extremely small. You would need a powerful microscope just to see it.

Do you want to hear a little more? The tiniest musical instrument is a "nanoguitar" made from a single silicon crystal. Its six strings can be plucked with a microscopic tool. The guitar is much smaller than a strand of your hair. In fact, it is too small to be seen by the human eye, and the sounds it makes cannot be heard by the human ear!

The smallest thermometer in the world is so tiny you cannot even see it. Its tip is much thinner than a fingernail. It was made at a university in New York. It is used to measure the temperature of single living cells.

The smallest map ever made was created in Zurich, Switzerland, by using electricity to rearrange single atoms. The map shows the entire

Western Hemisphere and is one-fiftieth as wide as a human hair. Try reading that map to find your way!

A laser beam is a very narrow, powerful beam of light. Different kinds of laser beams can be used to play music, read price codes, and cut metal. Some beams are thin enough to drill 200 holes on a spot as tiny as the head of a pin!

Looking for a quick read? You may want to check out a miniature book. Most miniature books are no more than 3 inches (7.5 centimeters) long. They can fit in the palm of your hand. Miniature books have been around since the 1400's. Early ones were handwritten, and some had beautifully detailed paintings.

What is the smallest dog? It is the Chihuahua. This dog is about 5 inches (13 centimeters) tall at its shoulder and weighs about 6 pounds (3 kilograms).

It will not take you long to travel down the world's shortest river. It is the Roe, in Montana. It is only 201 feet (61 meters) long, less than half a city block.

Ride to the end of the line on the world's shortest subway. The Istanbul Metro in Turkey is only 2,133 feet (650 meters) long.

You can cross the world's shortest boundary at La Linea, between Gibraltar and Spain. The border there is 1 mile (1.6 kilometers) long.

Would you like to tour the tiniest countries? The smallest is Vatican City, which is only 1/4 square mile (0.6 square kilometer), less than the length of two football fields. The next smallest are Monaco, about 3/4 square mile (1.8 square kilometers), and Nauru, a Pacific island nation of only about 8 square miles (21 square kilometers).

Compare the size of these countries to the size of your town. Ask your parents to help you

The red line on the map shows the boundary of Vatican City. In the photo, you can see the domed St. Peter's Church and St. Peter's Square. The two sites span nearly half the length of the world's smallest country.

figure out what is 1/4 mile (0.6 kilometer) north from your home, south, east, and west.

Australia looks like an island, but it is a continent. It is the smallest of the seven continents.

If you want smooth sailing, do not sail the smallest ocean. The Arctic Ocean is only 5 million square miles (14 million square kilometers), but most of it is ice. It would take twelve Arctic Oceans to fill the largest ocean, the Pacific.

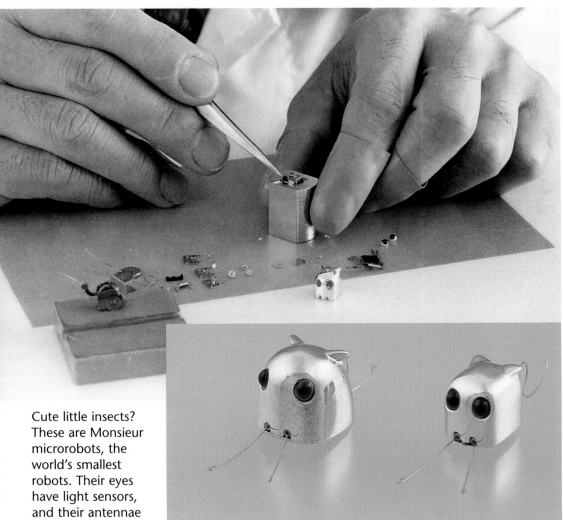

Cute little insects? These are Monsieur microrobots, the world's smallest robots. Their eyes have light sensors, and their antennae help in recharging. These tiny robots are put together mostly by hand!

The world's smallest robot is a prize-winning climber! The "Monsieur" microrobot, made in Japan, measures less than 6/100 cubic inch (0.9 cubic centimeter). It is made of about 95 watch parts and can move 24 inches (60 centimeters) per minute when it is fully charged.

The world's smallest submarine, built in England, is about 9 feet (3 meters) long, 4 feet (1.2 meters) wide, and 5 feet (1.5 meters) high. It can hold one person, dive about 100 feet (30 meters), and stay underwater four hours.

Imagine watching the slowest chess game ever played. It was in 1857 and was between Louis Paulsen from Germany and Charles Morphy from the United States. The game lasted 15 hours and ended in a draw. These days, clocks are used to limit playing time.

You can come in for a really low landing at the Schiphol Airport in Amsterdam, the Netherlands. It is the world's lowest international airport, 15 feet (4.6 meters) below sea level, the level of the world's oceans. The world's lowest road is along the Israeli shore of the Dead Sea. There, you would be strolling along at 1,290 feet (393 meters) below sea level!

WHY is that?

Many people in the Netherlands live below sea level. That is because most of the land was once covered by the ocean, lakes, and swamps. The people wanted more room to live so they filled in the watery areas and kept out more water with walls called dikes. These low land areas, called polders (POHL duhrz), are now cities and farms.

Fatal Facts

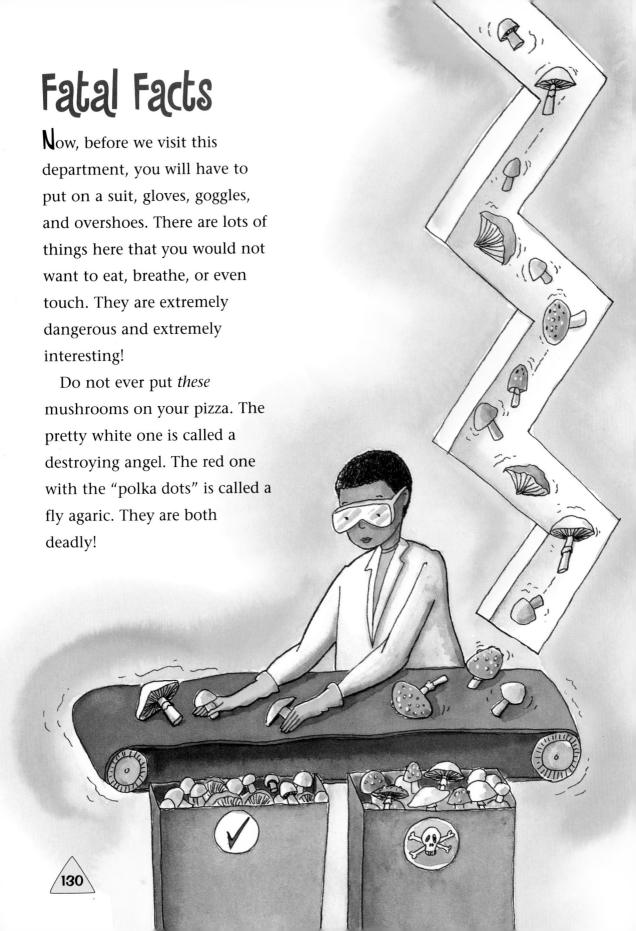

Now, before we visit this department, you will have to put on a suit, gloves, goggles, and overshoes. There are lots of things here that you would not want to eat, breathe, or even touch. They are extremely dangerous and extremely interesting!

Do not ever put *these* mushrooms on your pizza. The pretty white one is called a destroying angel. The red one with the "polka dots" is called a fly agaric. They are both deadly!

Do not eat strange berries, either. The belladonna plant is known as "deadly nightshade." Its berries are highly poisonous. But some other plants in the same family are good for you, including tomatoes, potatoes, and peppers.

Castor beans are not for nibbling. They too are poisonous. However, through special processes their oil is used to make medicine and paints.

destroying angel

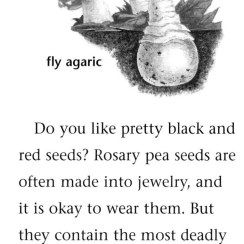

fly agaric

castor beans

Do you like pretty black and red seeds? Rosary pea seeds are often made into jewelry, and it is okay to wear them. But they contain the most deadly of all plant poisons. Eating a single seed could kill a person.

The stems of the rhubarb (ROO bahrb) plant make delicious pies. But do not use the leaves! They will make you ill if you swallow them.

rhubarb

Keep your gloves on! The skin of the golden poison arrow frog from western Colombia gives off the deadliest poison of any frog.

All sea snakes are poisonous. There's one that lives in the Timor Sea, in Indonesia, that has a venom 100 times more poisonous than any land snake.

Please make sure your goggles are secure. The African "spitting" cobra can squirt venom into the eyes of animals 8 feet (2.5 meters) away. The venom makes the eyes burn and can even cause blindness.

Keep your eyes open for fleas. One that lives on rats is infected with certain bacteria. Its bite spreads a terrible disease known as plague (playg). In the mid-1300's, the plague killed about 75 million people. Today, plague can be treated with medicine.

Poisonous but helpful

A pretty flowering plant called the foxglove has poisonous leaves. But the leaves can be carefully processed and used to make a heart medicine. The woody vine that makes a poison called curare (kyu RAH ree) is also helpful. In South America, people hunt animals with darts dipped in curare. Doctors also use a form of curare to relax patients during an operation.

Some diseases can be cured today, but wiping them out is hard. A bacteria causes tuberculosis. It can be treated with drugs, but over 3 million people die of it each year.

Little tropical water snails are one of the world's biggest health problems. They carry tiny worms called schistosomes (SHIHS tuh sohmz) that make people ill.

Did you know that so many plants and animals are poisonous? Well, it is only natural for them. These poisons help them survive and keep from being eaten.

Factory Fun

Find a Path to the Diamond!

The Fact Factory's Extreme Facts Department is full of fun, feats, and phenomena (fuh NOM uh nuh)! With a bit of luck, you can make your way past all of them to reach the Star of Africa diamond.

THINGS YOU NEED

- a die
- place markers
- a friend or two

RULES

- To decide who gets the first turn, both players should throw the die. Whoever rolls the higher number goes first.

- Throw the die to see how many spaces you should move forward.

- If you land on a space with special instructions, follow them.

- Whoever reaches the Star of Africa diamond first is the winner!

Slide down the world's lowest road, along the shore of the Dead Sea.

This space is guarded by the African spitting cobra. Return to your old space.

Traveling across Russia takes longer than expected. Miss a turn.

Move ahead by taking the Akashi Kaikyo bridge.

Skip through Vatican City and take a second turn.

Start

Fly forward 3 spaces with Kitti's hognose bat.

Use a laser beam to bore ahead! Take a second turn.

You're lost in the Chicxulub Basin. Miss a turn.

Climb the Great Wall of China and skip forward 3 spaces.

Get into a staring match with a giant squid. Miss a turn.

Hop into the *Thrust SSC* car. Zoom forward 6 spaces.

Wait for a three-toed tree sloth to move out of the way. Miss 2 turns.

Dive into the Roe River and move ahead 1 space.

Hurry past—belladonna plants are flourishing here! Keep going for another 5 spaces.

Climb ahead 3 spaces with the Monsieur microrobot.

A giant rafflesia blocks your way. Fall back 3 spaces to get your gas mask.

An Irish wolfhound steps on your place marker. Miss a turn.

Star of Africa diamond. You win!

Extreme Sports

Welcome to the farthest edge of the Fact Factory, where we like to push ourselves for fun! Hi, it's Zack Leigh So here. I come to this part of the Fact Factory to test myself and to see just how skillful, fit, and strong I really am. How do I do this? I do it by training for adventure races and extreme sports. Both activities make incredible demands of the people who take part in them.

Right now, I am training for an adventure race called the Eco-Challenge. In adventure races, teams compete against each other in a number of difficult events. One adventure race, for example, lasts for a week. First, the teams race each other on horses over 26 miles (40 kilometers). Team members take turns riding their horse and running alongside! Next, they swim through canyons of water. The next event is a hike, more than 100 miles (160 kilometers) across a desert. After the hike, teams climb up cliffs. Then, they raft down river rapids, where the water rushes quickly, and often over rocks. Finally, they paddle canoes across a lake for 50 miles (80 kilometers).

Obviously, this adventure race is extremely tough. Some racers have ended up in the hospital. Others thrive on such challenges.

People of all ages compete in adventure races. Helen Klein (*above*) completed the grueling Eco-Challenge when she was 72 years old.

Among those who have completed the race is a 72-year-old woman!

Another way I like to have fun is by climbing a mound or ridge of loose sand called a sand dune. Slogging over sand can be tough, can't it? I like to make it even tougher by wearing snowshoes. A snowshoe is made of a light, wooden frame with strips of leather stretched across it. People usually wear snowshoes to keep from sinking in deep, soft snow. This extreme sport, called sandshoeing, is a new twist on the popular Canadian sport of snowshoe running.

Other extreme sports take place on snow. People compete in skiboarding, for example, by gliding down snow-covered mountains on short, fat planks. As they zoom downward, they try to perform tricks, such as spinning on the planks.

Gliding swiftly over snow brings chills and thrills to some extreme sports enthusiasts.

Still other extreme sports take place indoors. Sport climbing, for example, is basically an indoor version of rock climbing. Inside a gym, sport climbers use only ropes to climb specially built walls. Traditional rock climbers, by contrast, use metal handholds and footholds nailed into the rocks. Sport climbers race each other to the top of the walls, which are between 45 and 60 feet (13.7 and 18.2 meters) tall. That's about as tall as a three- or four-story building!

Sport climbers use ropes to race each other to the top of a wall. The wall is indoors, but it's built like a rugged mountainside.

Some extreme sports are simply more daunting versions of everyday sports. Some skateboarders, for example, compete against each other in certain events. These include moving in the air over a U-shaped wall called a half pipe.

People who compete in bicycle stunts ride freestyle bikes up ramps and into the air. They try to twist and turn in various directions, while airborne!

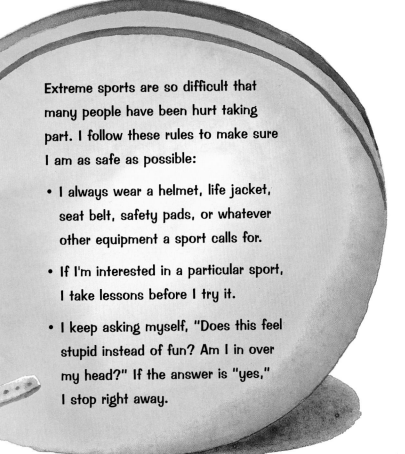

Extreme sports are so difficult that many people have been hurt taking part. I follow these rules to make sure I am as safe as possible:

• I always wear a helmet, life jacket, seat belt, safety pads, or whatever other equipment a sport calls for.

• If I'm interested in a particular sport, I take lessons before I try it.

• I keep asking myself, "Does this feel stupid instead of fun? Am I in over my head?" If the answer is "yes," I stop right away.

Scary Facts

It's that delicious tingle down your spine as you read a scary story. It's the slow spread of goosebumps as you swap ghost stories around the campfire. It's the thrilling *thump-thump-thump* of your heart as you watch a monster movie. Feeling scared can be lots of fun when you know you're really safe. So go ahead, scare yourself silly with some scary facts!

The Sky Is Falling

Over the centuries, many people have seen comets as signs of coming disaster, such as famine, disease, war, or destruction of the earth. Today, we know more about them. A comet's center is made of ice and dust, while its tail is made of dust or gas. Comets travel around the sun. They appear in the sky only when their path passes close to Earth. Halley's Comet is the most famous comet to be seen by people on Earth. Perhaps you and your family have seen comets move across our sky?

I'm so scared! And I'm not the only one. All the grown-ups are scared too. Last night, a strange star with a long tail appeared over our village. Nobody has ever seen a star like that before, not even my grandfather.

A star so odd must mean terrible things are going to happen. Papa and the other men went to check the crops. They were afraid the star might have caused them to fail. But everything was still growing—the wheat, the rye, and even the vegetables.

Now the men are worried that the star will bring a fierce storm. It could destroy the crops

before the harvest. If that happens, we will go hungry this winter.

I wanted to help Papa because I am big now, almost 9 years old. But Mama made me stay indoors with all my little brothers and sisters. She said the star may have stirred up sickness.

Mama and the other women have gone to church. They are praying that the star goes away and never comes back!

Frightful Lights

Oh, you spooked me, turning the page so fast! My name is Jenny. Sometimes people call me Jittery Jenny. Mom says there is no need to be scared, but I still get the jitters every once in a while. Why? Walk home with me, and I'll show you.

My friends and I need to walk past this big swamp to get home from the Fact Factory, and sometimes—look, there they are! See those tiny flames? They are coming right out of the ground! They are red, yellow, and sometimes blue.

Flames on the ground are creepy enough, but sometimes they leap from place to place. The

creepiest is when they float through the air.
If you try to get close, they vanish.

These lights have lots of names, such as
will-o'-the-wisp, jack-o'-lantern, fox fire, and
foolish fire. I have heard the fires are made by
a spirit that wants to make you lose your way.
Let's hurry home, and keep to the path!

*Will-o'-the-wisp looks ghostly, but it's perfectly
natural. Scientists think the flames are caused by
rotting plants. The plants give off marsh gas, or
methane (MEHTH ayn). When the gas gets trapped
in the pile of decay, it becomes very hot—hot
enough to start a fire and create the eerie flames.*

Ghoulish Facts

Creep down the clammy steps of ancient stone. Clutch the wall. Feel the cool slime ooze under your nails. Duck under the cobwebs and enter the Fact Factory's darkest corner.

My name is Morgan le Faye. I'm a magic woman from long ago. All the things we can't explain—mysteries—are filed in this shadowy part of the Fact Factory.

Are you surprised to see a statue of President Abraham Lincoln in this part of the Fact Factory? Believe it or not, Lincoln was interested in the supernatural. He and his wife, Mary, went to séances (SAY ahns uhz) after the deaths of their two young sons, Edward and Willie. They hoped to contact the spirits of the boys.

Early in April 1865, Lincoln had a nightmare. In his dream, he woke up to the sound of weeping in the White House. He wandered through empty rooms. Finally, he came to the East Room, where he saw soldiers guarding a coffin. Lincoln asked one of the soldiers who had died. The answer? "The President. He was killed by an assassin!"

On the evening of April 14, 1865, Lincoln attended a play at Ford's Theatre. A man named John Wilkes Booth pulled out a gun and shot the president in the head. The next day, Lincoln died.

Was Lincoln's dream a warning, or simply an eerie coincidence? What do you think?

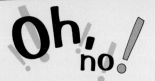

Eighty years ago two English girls, Elsie Wright and Frances Griffiths, said they had seen fairies. Better yet, they had photographed the tiny creatures! Many important people thought the fairies were real. But in fact, the girls had cut pictures of fairies from a book, placed them among the flowers, and photographed the pictures.

Now help me with this door. It leads to a special dock—the dock of the doomed. *CREEEEAK!* And there she is, a genuine ghost ship. She's called the *Mary Celeste*.

Some say the *Mary Celeste* was always an unlucky ship. Her name had been changed, from the *Amazon*. Sailors say that changing a ship's name brings bad luck, but that does not explain what happened to the *Mary Celeste*.

In November 1872, the ship set sail from New York to Genoa, Italy. She was carrying a cargo of alcohol. On board were the captain, his wife and child, and the crew.

A month later, another ship passed the *Mary Celeste* in the North Atlantic Ocean off the coast of Portugal. The *Mary Celeste* was deserted, its lifeboat missing.

Everyone had disappeared, apparently in a hurry. One man had started a letter to his wife, but broke off after four words. Sailors had left their pipes and tobacco behind. But why did they leave? Despite some torn sails—as if there had been a storm—the *Mary Celeste* was in better condition than most ships that crossed the Atlantic.

We still do not know. Some people think a giant squid attacked the ship. But the ship was not seriously damaged. Others think pirates killed everyone. But nothing of value was stolen. This is one mystery we will probably never solve. What do you think happened?

Fear—It's Physical

Ooooh! I'm the Fact Factory's pet poltergeist (POHL tuhr gyst), a ghost who makes lots of noise. I know a lot about scaring people. Look at what would have happened in your body if I scared you one night.

Danger!

First, nerve cells in your eyes would have sent an urgent message to your brain. And I mean urgent—the message would have traveled to your brain in less than a second!

Alert the entire body

Your brain would have analyzed the message and realized you were in danger. It would have sent its own message to different parts of your body. This message would have ordered them to release special substances called hormones (HAWR mohnz).

Focus, now

These hormones would have slowed down parts of your body that couldn't help you escape. Your digestion would have slowed down. There would have been less saliva in your mouth, and your mouth would have felt dry.

Prepare to fight

The pupils of your eyes would have gotten wider, and you could have seen me better. Your body would have released stored fats and sugars, and given you a surge of energy.

Prepare for flight

Your breathing would have gotten faster. Your heart would have beaten harder—*thump, thump, thump.* That way, it would have pumped more blood and energy to your legs, so that you could have run away. You might even have started to sweat, to keep your body cool.

The next time you get nervous or scared, take a deep breath. Your body is probably already preparing for fight or flight!

WHY is that?

The number 13 gives some people the jitters. They think the number is unlucky. Many trace this belief to Norse mythology in which 12 gods had been invited to a banquet. An uninvited evil god entered, making him the 13th guest, and killed one of the other gods. Others think the belief comes from the fact that 13 people sat at the Last Supper the night before Jesus Christ died. Also, witches' rituals supposedly require 13 people. Today, many hotels have no 13th floor. Elevators go straight from the 12th floor to the 14th!

From the Kid Fact Files

Name: Larry Champagne, III

Home: St. Louis, Missouri

Birthdate: April 17, 1985

Claim to Fame: A young hero

In a particularly scary situation, this young hero saved the day for his teacher and his classmates.

The morning of October 3, 1995, started off like any other school day for 10-year-old Larry Champagne, III. Larry and his brother were riding a school bus to Bellerive School, in St. Louis, Missouri, where Larry was in the fifth grade. About 20 other students were on the bus.

As the bus traveled along a busy highway, it suddenly lurched out of control. It bounced off two guard rails. A pickup truck crashed into it. Larry could see why. The bus driver had slipped from her seat. She was unconscious. No one was driving the bus!

Larry rushed to the driver's seat. His grandfather had taught him a little about driving. Larry grabbed the steering wheel, brought the bus under control, and hit the brake. The bus stopped. Larry and three other kids

Larry Champagne, III, young hero

opened the emergency doors so that everyone could get off the bus quickly. Five kids were slightly hurt, but everyone was alive.

It turned out the driver was very ill. Larry saved the lives of everyone on the bus. His courage and quick thinking won him the 1995 Young American Medal for Bravery. This medal is awarded by the United States Justice Department to young people who save lives. Larry Champagne, III, is a true hero!

Fearsome Phobias

We are all a little afraid of something, such as scuttling cockroaches, creaks in the night, or maybe even talking in front of a big group of people. Some people are *very* afraid. They are gripped by terror of a certain place or thing. These people have a phobia (FOH bee uh).

Can you match each of the phobias with what it means?

a. fear of heights
b. fear of open spaces
c. fear of small or closed-in spaces
d. fear of cats
e. fear of snakes
f. fear of spiders
g. fear of water
h. fear of dirt
i. fear of books
j. fear of laughter

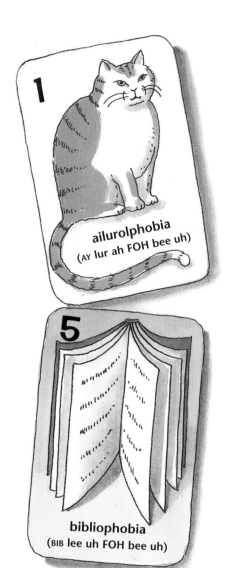

1

ailurolphobia
(AY lur ah FOH bee uh)

5

bibliophobia
(BIB lee uh FOH bee uh)

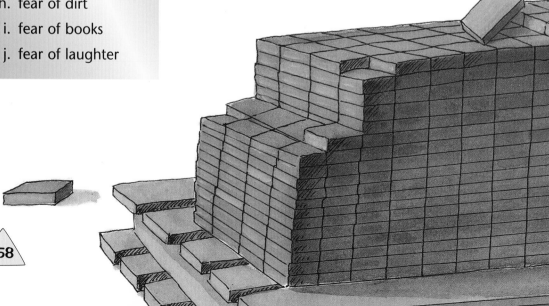

2 mysophobia
(MY suh FOH bee uh)

3 claustrophobia
(KLAWS truh FOH bee uh)

4 ophidiophobia
(oh FIH dee oh FOH bee uh)

6 agoraphobia
(AG uh ruh FOH bee uh)

7 geliophobia
(JEHL ee oh FOH bee uh)

8 arachnophobia
(uh RAK nuh FOH bee uh)

9 hydrophobia
(HY druh FOH bee uh)

10 acrophobia
(AK ruh FOH bee uh)

Many people can live with their phobias. Some things that cause phobias can simply be avoided. People who fear snakes or spiders, for example, stay away from places where they might see one. Other phobias make normal life nearly impossible. For example, people who fear open spaces may be afraid to leave their homes. Luckily, phobias can be cured. One way is to very gradually bring a fearful person into contact with the thing he or she fears. Over time the person becomes used to it, and it becomes less scary.

Quiet Creatures

A tarantula has a hairy body and looks fierce, but those found in the United States are quiet and live in burrows. Their bite is usually no more dangerous to people than the sting of a bee.

tarantula

Humor Conquers

If you have a fear that is not a phobia, maybe you can think of a fun way to control it. For example, if you are afraid of talking in front of a group of people, try pretending everyone in the audience is wearing only underwear! What else could you imagine?

False Alarms

Have you ever been frightened by a story in a book, a television show, or a movie in a theater? If so, you are not alone. Lots of people love a good scare. That's why this part of the Fact Factory is so popular.

This television is showing a frightening newscast that aired on March 20, 1983. Protesters had taken over parts of the city of Charleston, in South Carolina. The protesters demanded that all nuclear bombs in the area be disarmed (made harmless). Otherwise, they would explode their own nuclear bomb.

Thousands of panic-stricken viewers called the TV station, wanting to know more. In fact, the "newscast" was actually a television movie called "Special Bulletin." The TV station ran messages during the movie, telling viewers that it was fiction. But it looked real, so people got scared anyway!

Over here is the Factory's movie theater. It is usually showing *The Great Train Robbery*, a film made in 1903. It was the first movie to tell a story. The film was only about 11 minutes long, but it contained a scene of pure terror. In the scene, a bandit points a gun at the audience and shoots. Some viewers were so startled that they wanted to fight back.

Today, the theater is playing a movie by master of gimmicks William Castle. In the 1950's and 1960's, Castle created devices to scare the pants off movie audiences in the United States. For example, when a scary skeleton appeared in one movie, a larger-than-life plastic skeleton emerged from a box next to the screen. It floated above viewers' heads on an invisible wire. Yikes!

Another movie of Castle's literally made viewers' bodies tingle. The movie was about a Tingler that lives in some people's spines. To get rid of the Tingler, the person must scream when scared. Before this movie was shown, special equipment was installed under each seat. Each time the Tingler appeared on screen, the projectionist pushed a button, and viewers got a gentle shock. The audience would think that the Tingler was loose in the theater!

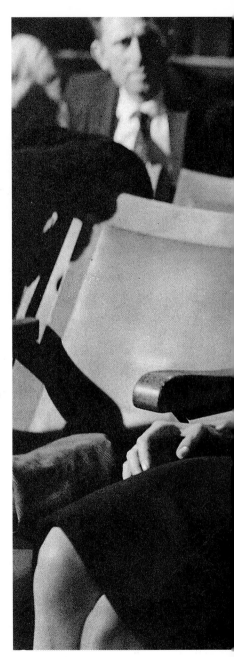

Careful where you sit! The chairs in this theater are equipped to shock the audience whenever the Tingler appears on screen. Or is the Tingler really loose in the theater?

Plays may seem tame by comparison, but they can scare people too. A play called *The Strange Case of Dr. Jekyll and Mr. Hyde* chilled London audiences in 1888. The story is about a good man, Dr. Jekyll, who drinks a potion and turns into the evil Mr. Hyde. The actor, Richard Mansfield, was convincing as Mr. Hyde—too convincing. Many people called the police, insisting that Mansfield was actually a man wanted for terrible murders. Mansfield had to close the play early.

Fifty years later, a radio play called *War of the Worlds* caused an uproar in the United States. The play was made up of news reports about Martians invading New Jersey. Many listeners thought the Martians were really attacking. Thousands called the police. Many fled their homes. Others were treated for shock.

You could say that all these works of fiction were a howling success. So remember, always try to keep straight what is fact and what is fake!

When Orson Welles *(above)* aired his play *War of the Worlds* on the radio, many people believed that Martians were really invading New Jersey.

WHY is that?

Many actors never refer to Shakespeare's play *Macbeth* by its name. They believe that the play is cursed, and that anyone who speaks its name will have bad luck. They call it by other names, such as *the Scottish play* or simply *that play*.

How Frankenstein Came to Be

Do you know the story of Frankenstein, the *real* Frankenstein? Lots of movies have been made about Frankenstein, but most don't tell the real story.

Frankenstein is a creepy book about a scientist named Dr. Frankenstein. He thinks he is so smart he can do anything. He wants to create a living being.

Dr. Frankenstein gathers body parts and pieces them together to make a tall, handsome creature. Then he zaps the creature with electricity. The creature shudders and opens his eyes. He is alive! But he is so ugly that Dr. Frankenstein runs away.

The creature is very smart and loving, but everyone hates him because he is so ugly. He asks Frankenstein to make him a wife, so that he won't be so lonely.

At first, Frankenstein agrees. Then he goes back on his promise. Enraged, the creature becomes violent. Frankenstein dies trying to kill the creature. The creature disappears near the North Pole.

Frankenstein was the first science-fiction story. It is a serious story that warns us about the pain we cause when we judge others by their appearance. The author, Mary Shelley, was only 21 when she came up with the idea.

The idea for the story came to Mary when in 1816 she visited Switzerland with her husband, the great poet Percy Bysshe Shelley, and other family members. One of their neighbors, Lord Byron, was also a famous poet. The Shelleys and Lord Byron became friends.

That summer, it rained and rained and rained. The friends huddled indoors for days,

reading ghost stories by the fire. Then Byron had an idea: "We will each write a ghost story!"

The friends immediately began scribbling. Only Mary had no ideas. Every day the others asked, "Have you thought of a story?" And every day, she had to say, "No."

One evening, Mary listened as Shelley and Lord Byron chatted. They talked about all the new things scientists were learning. They wondered if people would someday learn how to create life. Perhaps they could bring a dead body back to life!

That night, Mary couldn't sleep. Pictures swirled through her mind. A scientist kneeling beside a body he had put together. The creature stirring. The scientist running away. The creature standing over the sleeping scientist.

"I opened (my eyes) in terror. The idea so possessed my mind, that a thrill of fear ran through me," she said later.

Mary had her story at last. It thrilled her friends the next day. Percy Shelley insisted she write it down. Mary wanted her story "to make the reader dread to look round, to curdle the blood, and quicken the beatings of the heart." She got her wish!

Factory Fun

Write a Fright!

If you like to read scary stories, why not try to write one of your own? Our fact-checkers here at the Fact Factory are always rummaging through the files, adding facts, and weeding out fiction.

Maybe you have had a scare that you can turn into a story. Or, try looking through some of the tidbits we have tossed. Maybe they will help you make up your own tale of science fiction or the supernatural.

THINGS YOU NEED

a pencil or pen

lots of paper

1 What happens in your story? Let's look through our out-box for ideas.

- Someone goes back in time or zooms into the future.
- Someone travels light-years through space.
- People or things mysteriously disappear.
- Someone gets lost or trapped in a creepy place.

2 Who appears in your story? In a scary story, you don't have to stick to humans!

- The Loch Ness monster is a huge, mysterious water animal that supposedly lurks in a Scottish lake.

- Bigfoot, or Sasquatch, is a large, hairy, manlike creature said to roam North America.

- Yeti, or the Abominable Snowman, is a giant being that may hide in the Himalaya.

3 Finally, where does your story take place? Ah, here's a pile of scary settings:

- Outer space—in a spaceship or in a new world

- Towns that people have deserted for a mysterious reason

- A gloomy castle, complete with secret passageways, dungeons, and towers

You can probably think up lots of other scary events, creatures, and places. Write them down before you forget! Then, tell them to your friends one dark night.

Facts About Fun Stuff

Movies, music, sports, and more—
we at the Fact Factory have the
facts on the fun stuff!

Screen and Stage Facts

People around the world watch a lot of television. In fact, children in the United States and Europe watch about 20 hours of television a week. Do you think that's too much? How much do you watch?

When you do view TV you probably do so in the comfort of your own home. In the countryside of India, however, most families cannot afford TV sets. Children in those areas watch TV with their families and neighbors in village community centers, where everyone shares a set.

In the countryside of India, most people do not have a TV in their home. They watch TV in a village center.

John Baird invented this television system in 1925. Imagine trying to watch your favorite television show on a screen as little as this one.

TV is so popular now throughout the world that it may seem hard to believe it's only been around about 75 years. The first public demonstration of a mechanical television system was in 1925, by Scottish inventor John Baird. Vladimir K. Zworykin, a Russian-born American scientist, demonstrated the first completely electronic, practice television system in 1929.

The first images shown on TV were not very exciting. They included a galloping horse and a picture of a dollar sign. When television programming began in New York, programs were so rare that viewers got a postcard telling them when a program would be on!

Movies were born about 30 years before television. Believe it or not, a small café in Paris was probably the world's first movie theater. The Lumière brothers showed the first film to the public there in 1895. Only 35 people showed up, but the new art form soon caught on.

You would probably find old movies very strange because they were black and white, as well as silent. There were no sound effects, and the actors did not speak. Instead, words were flashed on the screen explaining what the actors were saying.

Today, of course, sound helps us believe what we see on the screen. Have you ever watched a monster movie where a giant critter stomped on cars or toppled buildings? Don't believe everything you hear! The sounds of squishing and other destruction may actually be the work of artists who create noises in a studio.

Here is a quick quiz question: Where is the world's busiest film studio? Surprise, it's not Hollywood! Filmmakers in India turn out about 900 movies a year, about three times as many as the United States.

This movie isn't being filmed in Hollywood, but it is being shot in the movie capital of the world—India. India produces several hundred films each year.

From the Kid Fact Files

Name: *Shirley Temple*

Home: *Woodside, California*

Birthdate: *April 23, 1928*

Claim to Fame: *Child movie star and U.S. ambassador*

From the Kid Fact Files comes this story of a young actress who grew up entertaining the masses and throughout her life served as a positive role model.

Life was very hard for families during the 1930's. Many parents lost their jobs. Without work, they were too poor to buy food. Children had to stand in lines to receive free bread and soup. During this terrible time, a young girl did the impossible—she cheered people up.

Shirley Temple was only 3 years old when she started singing, dancing, and acting in movies. Her cheerful personality, dimpled smile, and mop of curly hair won the hearts of moviegoers. By the time Shirley was 6, she was a star. In 1935, when girls across America were asked who they would most like to be, Shirley was their number-one choice!

In her movies, Shirley sang and danced with African Americans. In the 1930's, most white actresses did not

Shirley Temple and dance partners in "Little Miss Broadway"

do this. Shirley usually played girls who overcame problems. In "Heidi," for example, she plays a girl who fights to return to her mountain home after she is tricked into moving to a city.

Between 1935 and 1938, Shirley was one of America's top movie stars. In 1934, she won a special Academy Award. She stopped making movies when she was 21.

Shirley married Charles A. Black and raised three children. Later, she became the U.S. ambassador to the United Nations, Ghana, and Czechoslovakia. An ambassador represents the U.S. President overseas and tries to settle arguments with other countries. Onscreen and off, Shirley made the world better. Today, kids can enjoy her films by watching them on video.

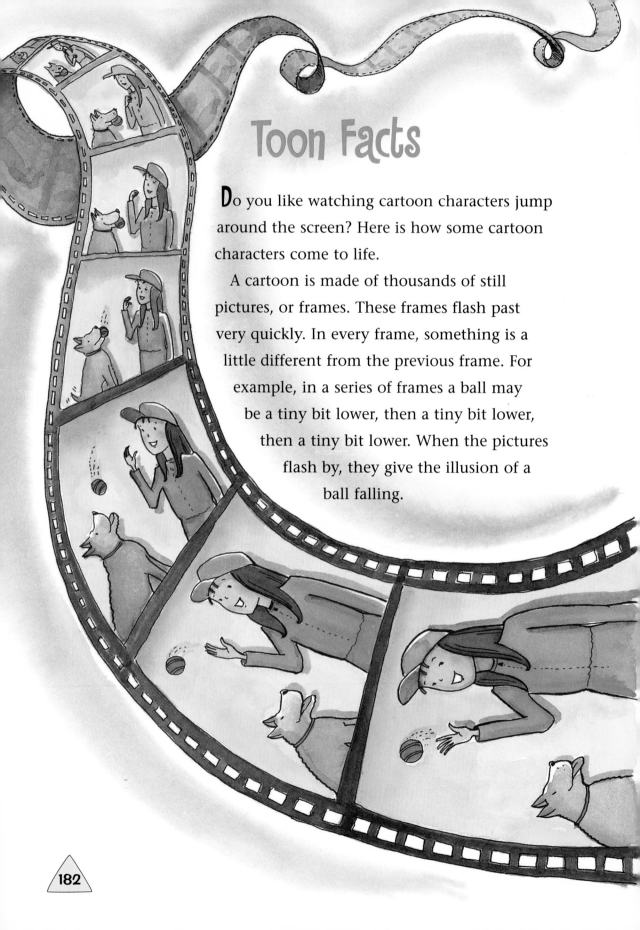

Toon Facts

Do you like watching cartoon characters jump around the screen? Here is how some cartoon characters come to life.

A cartoon is made of thousands of still pictures, or frames. These frames flash past very quickly. In every frame, something is a little different from the previous frame. For example, in a series of frames a ball may be a tiny bit lower, then a tiny bit lower, then a tiny bit lower. When the pictures flash by, they give the illusion of a ball falling.

Cel animation

Cel animation is the technique used to make many animated cartoons. Here are the steps needed to make the thousands of frames needed for a cartoon.

1. An artist draws the background scenery for the film. The backgrounds include everything except the characters.

2. The animator draws the characters. This artist must create a series of drawings for each movement made by a character.

3. Other artists trace the animator's drawings in ink onto transparent sheets called cels.

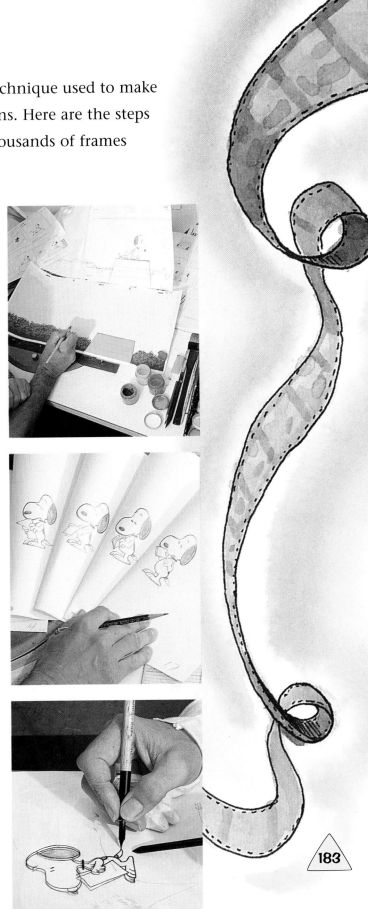

183

4. Artists paint the cels with the colors needed for each character. They paint on the reverse side of the cel.

5. Each cel is laid over the right background scenery and photographed one frame at a time.

Because hand-drawn cartoons take so much work and are expensive to make, they nearly died out in the 1970's. But in the 1980's and 1990's, several hit movies and popular TV shows were cartoons. This is in part thanks to computers. Today, computers are sometimes used to color, shade, and move drawings. This technique is called computer animation. Artists create the drawings on a display screen. The process is often quicker than drawing by hand.

Computers are used to create complicated shading and 3-D effects that make animations amazingly lifelike. The ants shown on the next page appear to have human facial expressions.

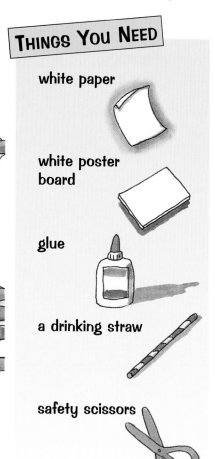

Factory Fun

Make Pictures Move!

The thaumatrope (THAW muh trohp) was a toy that delighted children in the 1820's. A thaumatrope was a disk with one picture on the front and another on the back. If you twirled the disk quickly, the pictures merged into one, just as they do in cartoons! See for yourself by making this version of the thaumatrope.

THINGS YOU NEED

white paper

white poster board

glue

a drinking straw

safety scissors

1 Draw four circles, all the same size. Draw two of the circles on the paper and two on the poster board.

2 Cut out the circles.

3 On each paper circle, draw a different picture. For example, draw a bird on one and a cage on the other.

4 Glue each paper circle onto a circle of poster board.

5 Glue the straw to the back of one drawing, so that it looks like a kind of lollipop.

6 Glue the backs of the two drawings together. You should have a kind of sandwich, with the straw lying between two circles of poster board. Let the thaumatrope dry.

7 Hold the straw between the palms of your hands. Rub your palms back and forth, twirling the straw and making the circles move rapidly. How many pictures do you see?

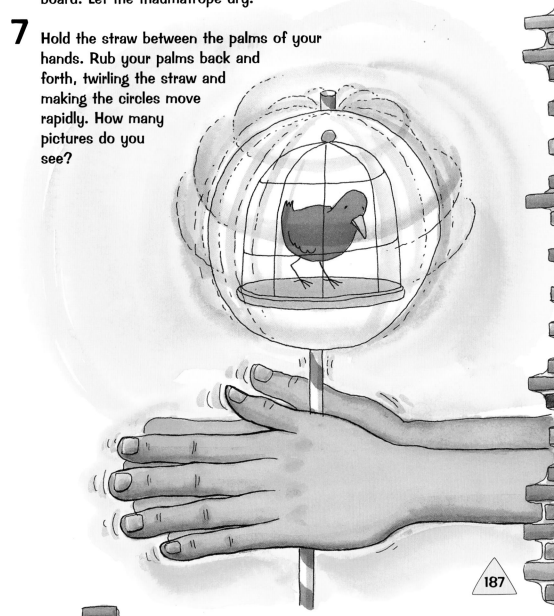

Factory Closeouts

Dear Customer:

The Fact Factory is clearing out its attic. We need to get rid of these fun items that were wildly popular in the 1970's and 1980's. No reasonable offer will be refused!

Bat boredom with Pong!

Get ready for some 1972 thrills! Pong, one of the first successful video games, is a nerve-racking way to play tennis on your TV. A short line on the screen acts as your racket. Hit the ball back and forth for hours! Are you having fun yet?

Bye-bye, batteries!

Invented in 1982, this clock does not plug into the wall. It plugs into potatoes! By sticking electrodes into two potatoes, you set off a chemical reaction that creates electricity. No one can call this idea half-baked.

Watch TV—on your wrist!

Now for 1983, this television has a flat screen so thin you can wear it on your wrist, just like a wristwatch. In fact, the screen may look a lot like the face of your digital watch because it uses a liquid crystal display. As a result, the picture is a little murky, dull, and fuzzy. Well, you can't have everything!

A sound device!

You cannot go wrong with this light switch invented in 1984. It turns on any lamp as soon as it "hears" the slightest sound. Would you say that was a bright idea?

What's the Good Word?

Welcome to the Fact Factory's Word Room! This is where every word gets to tell its story, so the chattering and nattering is nonstop. My name's Libby Rarian, and I love working here.

English has more words than any other language, more than 600,000 total. Plus, words keep sneaking in from other languages. In fact, probably more than half of our total vocabulary comes from other languages.

Pal came from the Romany language spoken by Gypsies. *Tea* came from Chinese, and *school* came from Greek. In Greek, the word *school* originally meant "leisure"!

Yo-yo was taken from the Filipino language. But in the

1920's, an American businessman patented the toy and claimed he created the word. He sued a business rival for using the word *yo-yo*. But his rival came from the Philippines and proved that the word did too. Case dismissed!

WHY is that?

The words *lonely*, *gnarl*, and *immediacy* are part of English, thanks to playwright William Shakespeare. These are just a few of the words he made up.

Cover your ears if you pass any closets. That's where we lock up all the slang and other words that are not used in formal English. For example, *ain't* was once put forward as a short way of saying *am not*. But *ain't* is still not considered proper English. What slang words do you know?

Today, there are about 6,000 languages in the world. Many of those languages have very few speakers. Only about 350 Indians living in Colombia speak the Tatuyo (tah TOO yoh) language, for example. Mandarin Chinese has the most speakers—more than 850 million in all!

Watch your tone of voice if you speak Chinese. In this language, words change meaning with the tone of your voice. If you say *ma,* you can mean "mother," "horse," or "scold," depending on your tone.

In the Hopi Indian language, you will find "boy words" and "girl words." If you want to say "thank you," say *KWAH kwy* if you are a boy, and *ehs KWAH lee* if you are a girl.

Language can tell us a lot about people's way of life. In the Arabic language, there is only one word for both *snow* and *ice.* But there are several words for *camel!* Why do you think that is?

Speak a secret language!

Want a secret language that only you and your friends can understand? Try making up a rhyming slang. For example, you could use the word *curl* for *girl.* Or try saying words backward.

ma ma ma ma ma ma ma ma ma

ma

ma

mother

horse

scold

Chatty gorilla

A female gorilla called Koko has learned sign language. Koko uses several hundred signs to talk to humans.

Now let's move on to the Fact Factory's library. Do you like to read stories and poems? Until the 1700's, youngsters could choose mainly from three kinds of books: schoolbooks, religious books, and books that warned children to behave—or else!

Books have changed since then. The books you love today may have thrilled your great-great-great-great-great-grandparents too! Take *Robinson Crusoe* and *Gulliver's Travels*. These books were actually written for adults in the 1700's, but children have loved these adventure stories ever since.

Probably the favorite children's book of all time is *Alice's Adventures in Wonderland*. It was written by England's Lewis Carroll in 1865. He did not set out to write a book. He started telling the story while picnicking with friends, to amuse a little girl named Alice.

FAST

PAGE-TURNING SPEED

SLOW

a. soft drink

b. private school

c. small grocery

d. marble

e. corn

f. handsome child

g. good man

h. cooler

Is that English?

English varies around the world. Listed here are words often used by certain English-speakers. Can you match them with another English word or phrase used by others to describe the same thing? What words do you use?

1. braw bairn (Scotland)
2. public school (England)
3. mineral (Ireland)
4. milk bar (Australia)
5. dag (New Zealand)
6. mealie (South Africa)
7. chilly bin (Bahamas)
8. glassy (Belize)

Ancient Art at Altamira

Thousands of years ago, before there were written words, people used art to record their thoughts and feelings. Here's the story of a little girl who found some of these paintings over 100 years ago.

Hello, my name is Maria. Do you know much about art? I didn't when I was a little girl, but that is when I made a great art discovery!

At that time, in the 1870's, scientists were starting to learn about ancient people who had lived in caves. My Papa, Marcelino Sanz de Sautuola, thought that such early people may have lived near our home in Spain, in a cave called Altamira (UHL tuh MEER uh). In 1877, we set out together to search the cave.

Papa dug the cave floor, hoping to find tools or carvings made by the cave dwellers. I held candles for him so he could see in the dark. One day in 1879, when I was 8, I went exploring by myself. That's when I saw them up on the ceiling. Hoofs. Tails. Bodies. Horns. Huge and powerful, red and black. "Look, Papa!" I called. "Bulls!"

Papa thought the cave dwellers had painted these magnificent animals. He wrote down and published the discovery for others to read about. But outside Spain, leading

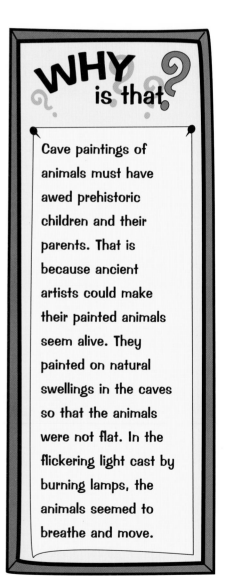

WHY is that?

Cave paintings of animals must have awed prehistoric children and their parents. That is because ancient artists could make their painted animals seem alive. They painted on natural swellings in the caves so that the animals were not flat. In the flickering light cast by burning lamps, the animals seemed to breathe and move.

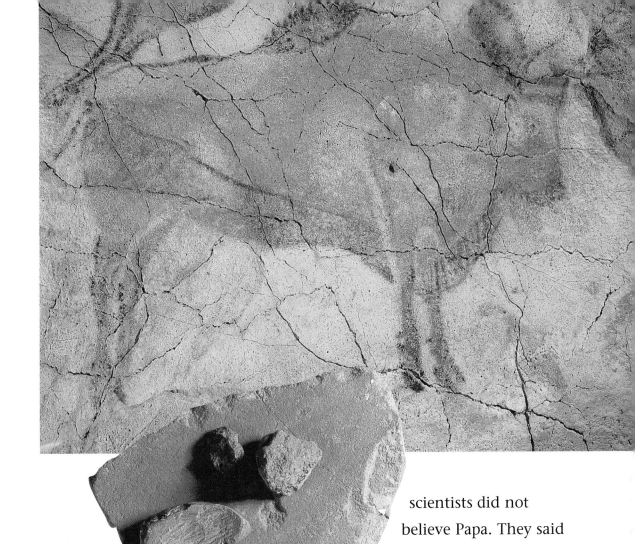

Ice Age artists drew the bison *(top)* on the walls and ceilings at Altamira. These small pieces of ocher *(above)* may have been used as crayons.

scientists did not believe Papa. They said early people could never have created such wonders.

Later, people found similar paintings in other caves. Finally, 23 years after my discovery, the experts admitted they were wrong about Altamira. Today we know that the paintings are about 15,000 years old. They were probably made from natural colors from clay, charcoal, or minerals. I was the first person to see the paintings in thousands of years!

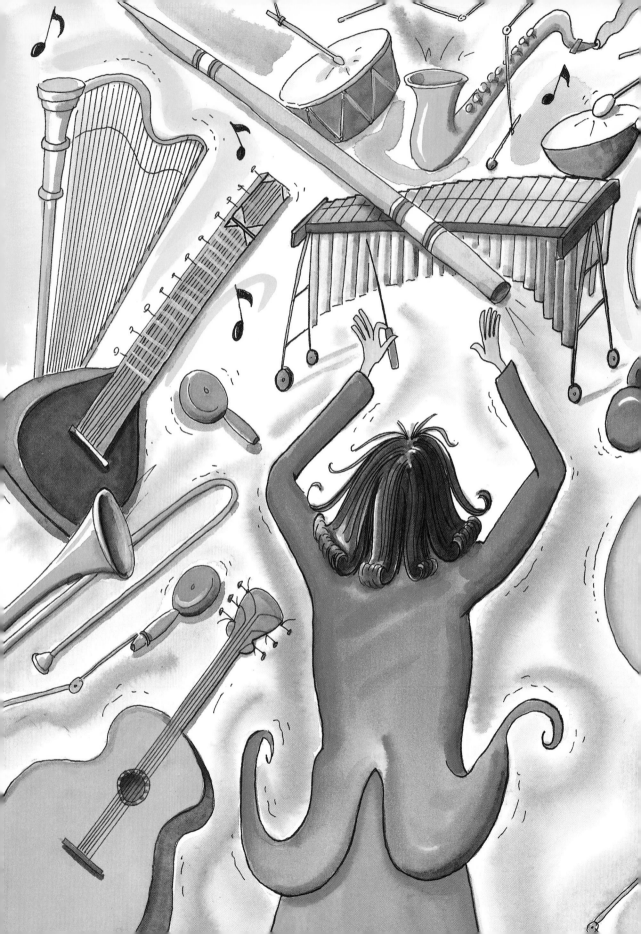

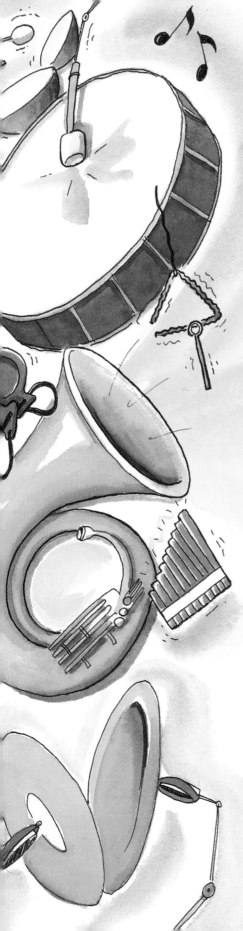

Music, Maestro!

Hello. Bea Leevit here. Weird vibes are in the air in this part of the Fact Factory. They come from a force of great power. This force can reach into your soul and change your deepest feelings. It can bring a lump to your throat, a spring to your step, or a smile to your face. What is this awesome force? It's music.

Nobody knows when or how music began. But we know it is one of the oldest arts. A flute found in a cave in Slovenia is at least 43,000 years old.

Every culture has its own kind of music. Most religions use music during services to inspire feelings of wonder. Instruments are never used in Muslim services though. Instead, worshipers make their own music by chanting prayers.

How important is music in your daily life? Do you use it mainly as background entertainment? In Africa, every event in a child's life, including being born, getting a first tooth, and growing up, is marked with a song.

Many Native Americans believe music can heal the sick, change the weather, or help them in other ways. Children in the Nez Perce tribe used to go into the wilderness, hoping that a spirit would appear in a dream. The spirit, usually an animal, would sing a message about its special power. A girl who dreamed of a blackbird, for example, would receive healing power from that spirit.

A lot of modern music has its roots in the music of African Americans. When Africans were taken from their homes and brought to America as slaves, they brought their music with them. The rhythms of that music are a big part of popular music.

Blues singers often sing about hard times. The sad wail of blues comes partly from an African style of singing. One person would sing out, and another would sing in response.

Blues helped give birth to jazz, the first kind of popular music that appealed to all kinds of people. Jazz singers, like blues singers, sang of sad things. But the music also made people dance and feel better! Today, many people agree that jazz is the only original art form that is truly American.

Drums are the most important instruments in African music. Some are made of animal skins, and others from hollowed logs.

Jazz music mixes African beats with American and European combinations of musical notes, or harmony.

Many parents worried about the way teen-age girls reacted to the famous rock band the Beatles.

Rock music borrowed from blues and jazz, as well as from country and western music. When rock began in the 1950's, it shocked many parents. They did not like the way singer Elvis Presley wiggled his hips to music. In fact, when he was first on TV, cameras only filmed him from the waist up. Later in the 1960's, parents worried about the way teen-age girls screamed, sobbed, and fainted at the Beatles' concerts. Since the 1980's, one of the most important things to hit rock

music has been rap music. Rap uses music in new ways. For example, rappers tend to chant or speak rapidly to music, rather than sing. Rap songs sometimes use snatches of old songs. This is called sampling. Some rap artists grab a spinning record and move it back and forth under the needle, creating new sounds. This is called scratching.

Many rap songs describe serious problems, especially in inner cities. But some critics say rap lyrics encourage violence, or put down women and other groups. What do you think?

WHY is that?

Music from other cultures may sound weird to you. That is because you are used to hearing certain sounds in music. Music in Europe and North America often blends three or more notes at the same time. We call this harmony. Also, this music is often based on a series of eight musical notes. You can probably sing this series, called a scale: *doh, re, mi, fah, so, la, ti, doh.* But Chinese music uses a different scale and no harmony. So, it might sound strange to your ears.

Chime in with Music

People have made music with chimes for thousands of years. Stone chimes, for example, were used in the Far East more than 4,000 years ago. Today, the chimes used in orchestras are made of 18 to 20 brass or steel tubes hung on a frame. You can make your own chimes with just eight glasses of water and a teaspoon!

THINGS YOU NEED

8 glasses, the thinner the better (Ask your parents for permission!)

water

a teaspoon and measuring cups

food coloring (optional)

1 Line up the glasses. Fill one with 2 2/3 cups of water. This will be the lowest note, *doh*.

2 Put 2 1/3 cups of water in the next glass. This will be *re* (ray).

3 Put 2 cups of water in the next glass. This will be *mi* (mee).

4 Put 1 2/3 cups of water in the next glass. This will be *fah*.

5 Put 1 1/3 cups of water in the next glass. This will be *so* (soh).

6 Put 1 cup of water in the next glass. This will be *la* (lah).

7 Put 2/3 cup of water in the next glass. This will be *ti* (tee).

8 Put 1/3 cup of water in the next glass. This will be the highest note, also called *doh.*

9 Add food coloring to the water to make your chimes pretty. To sound the notes, tap the rim of each glass gently with the teaspoon. Can you tap out a tune?

By filling the glasses with different amounts of water, you can sound a series of notes— *doh, re, mi, fah, so, la, ti, doh*—called a scale. Most American and European music is based on this scale.

So Sport, What Do You Know?

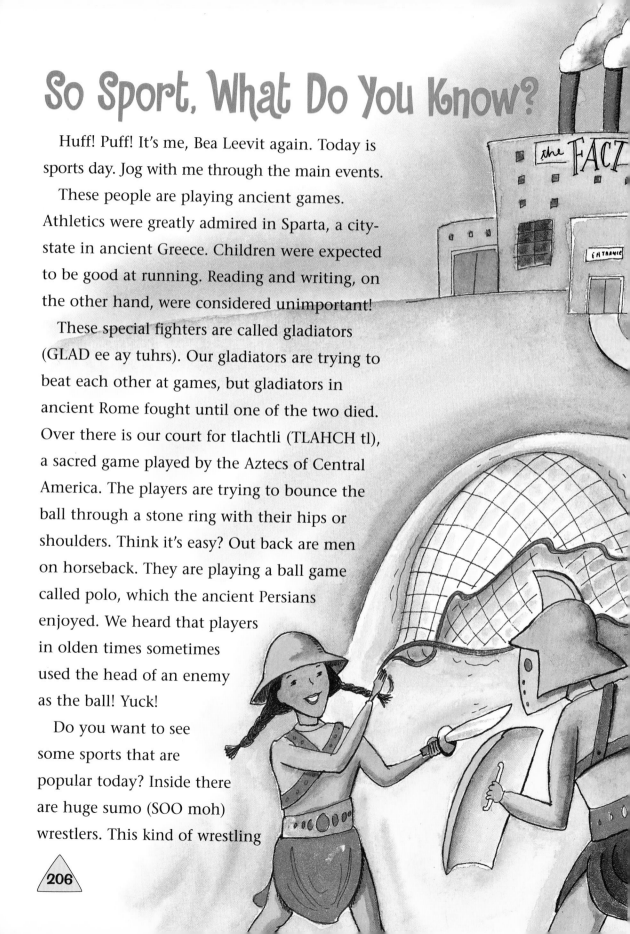

Huff! Puff! It's me, Bea Leevit again. Today is sports day. Jog with me through the main events.

These people are playing ancient games. Athletics were greatly admired in Sparta, a city-state in ancient Greece. Children were expected to be good at running. Reading and writing, on the other hand, were considered unimportant!

These special fighters are called gladiators (GLAD ee ay tuhrs). Our gladiators are trying to beat each other at games, but gladiators in ancient Rome fought until one of the two died. Over there is our court for tlachtli (TLAHCH tl), a sacred game played by the Aztecs of Central America. The players are trying to bounce the ball through a stone ring with their hips or shoulders. Think it's easy? Out back are men on horseback. They are playing a ball game called polo, which the ancient Persians enjoyed. We heard that players in olden times sometimes used the head of an enemy as the ball! Yuck!

Do you want to see some sports that are popular today? Inside there are huge sumo (SOO moh) wrestlers. This kind of wrestling

is a favorite sport in Japan. Sumo wrestlers try to force each other to the floor or outside a circle. Another game called the blanket toss is played by the Inuit people, who live near the North Pole. One person sits on the blanket. A group pulls the blanket tight, tossing the person into the air. That person tries to land upright on the blanket.

The sports-day event that has the most fans is the soccer match! Soccer, which is called football in many countries, is the world's favorite sport. People in China played the earliest form of this game, called tsu chu, more than 2,000 years ago. In England, the game became part of festivals held the day before Lent began. Hundreds of players chased the ball through the streets, hurting people and wrecking property. In disgust, England's kings and queens banned soccer. But people liked the game so much, they kept playing anyway, often in churchyards, where the government had no authority. Today, it is still that country's number-one sport!

Did you know that basketball is now the world's most popular indoor sport? A teacher in Massachusetts invented it in 1891. The first players used a soccer ball and peach baskets!

Now here is a favorite event of young people—skateboarding. Did you

know that skateboarding grew out of surfing? Surfing is an old sport, developed by the ancient Hawaiians, while skateboarding is only 60 years old. But both sports demand the same skills: great balance, exact timing, and quick reflexes.

Skateboarding is not the only sport to come from another sport. During the 1700's, Americans played an English bat-and-ball game called rounders. They changed the rules so much it became a new game—baseball!

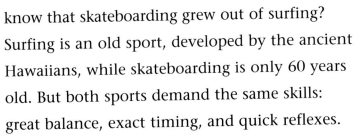

WHY is that?

Why do so many people like to play and watch sports? No one knows for sure, but one theory is that sport takes the place of hunting in people's lives today. In the past, people spent much of their day running, jumping, and climbing as they hunted for food. Today, most people do not hunt for food, so they "hunt" for goals, baskets, and touchdowns instead!

Many outstanding young athletes have thrilled sports fans around the world. In 1958, for example, a small 17-year-old boy caused an uproar in Brazil. He won a place on the nation's soccer team. The team was about to compete in the World Cup. How could a boy so young play in the world's most important soccer competition? Fans did not need to worry. The teen-ager, Pelé (peh LAY), helped Brazil win the World Cup. Pelé is still the only soccer player ever to score 1,000 goals during his career. In fact, he scored 1,281.

People who watched the 1976 Olympics could not take their eyes off 14-year-old gymnast Nadia Comaneci (NAH dee uh koh mah NEECH). As the Romanian girl swung and turned on the

WHY is that?

Most people think Babe Didrikson Zaharias (DIHD rihk suhn zuh HAYR ee uhs) was the best female athlete ever. Why? Because Babe excelled at many sports, including golf, track and field, basketball, baseball, pocket billiards, tennis, swimming, and diving. In a contest held to choose U.S. athletes for the 1932 Olympic Games, Babe set four world records in three hours. At the Olympics, she set three more!

bars, she did not make a single mistake. Nadia was the first gymnast ever to earn a score of 10.00, a perfect score. And before the games ended, Nadia received seven perfect scores!

Two young golfers the world likes to watch are Tiger Woods and Se Ri Pak. American Tiger Woods won the Masters Tournament in 1997, when he was 21. In 1998, Se Ri Pak of South Korea won the U.S. Women's Open when she was 20. Tiger and Se Ri were the youngest golf champs ever!

Tiger Woods

Glossary

Here are some words you have read in this book. You can see how to say them in parentheses after the word—for example, **archaeologist** (AHR kee AHL uh jihst). Say the parts in small letters more softly, those in small capital letters a little louder or with a little more emphasis, and those in large capital letters loudest or with the most emphasis. Following the pronunciation are one or two sentences that tell the meaning of the word as it is used in this book.

Academy Award (uh CAD uh mee uh WARD)
An award given for outstanding work for a movie. Academy Awards are also known as Oscars.

acid rain (AS ihd rayn)
Polluted rain that damages statues, buildings, and soil. It kills water life. Acid rain harms trees, lakes, rivers, and streams.

allergic (uh LUHR jihk)
Having a negative reaction to something that one eats, drinks, or breathes. People who are allergic to something may sneeze, have watery eyes, or break out in a rash when they are near that thing.

ambassador (am BAS uh duhr)
A representative sent by a government to another country. An ambassador acts and speaks for his or her government in another country or before an organization.

archaeologist (ahr kee AHL uh jihst)
A person who learns about the people, customs, and life of long ago by finding and studying the remains of ancient cities and towns.

asteroid (AS tuhr oyd)
A very small object that revolves around the sun.

atmosphere (AT muh sfeer)
The layer of gases that surrounds Earth or another heavenly body. Such gases may include oxygen, nitrogen, and carbon dioxide.

atom (AT uhm)
The smallest bit into which a single chemical element, such as gold or oxygen, can be divided without changing it. All things are made of atoms.

bacteria (bak TIHR ee uh)
Kinds of simple living things so small that they can usually be seen only with a microscope. Some consist of only one cell.

carat (KAYR uht)
A measurement of weight of a diamond or other precious stone. It would take about 2,250 carats to make one pound.

continent (KAHN tuh nuhnt)
One of the seven great masses of land on Earth.

earthquake (URTH kwayk)
A shaking or sliding of the ground. An earthquake is caused by changes in the size and shape of rocks under the earth's surface.

electrode (ih LECH trohd)
A piece of metal through which electricity flows. A battery has two electrodes.

famine (FAM uhn)
A time of starving.

fossil (FAHS uhl)
The mark or remains of a plant or animal that lived thousands or millions of years ago.

fungus (FUHNG guhs)
A living thing that feeds on rotting matter or on other living things. A mushroom is a fungus. The plural is **fungi** (FUHN jy).

gnarl (NARL)
To make knotted, rugged, or twisted, like an old tree.

herb (uhrb or hurb)
A low-growing plant, often used to flavor food or used in medicines.

immediacy (ih MEE dee uh see)
Done without delay.

Inuit (IHN yoo iht)
A people who live in and near the Arctic.

lightning (LYT nihng)
A flash of light in the sky. Lightning is caused by electricity moving between clouds or between a cloud and the ground.

mammal (MAM uhl)
An animal that is warm blooded, has a backbone, and feeds its young on its mother's milk.

mercurial (muhr KYUHR ee uhl)
Changeable.

mortar (MAWR tuhr)
A building material that is used like cement to hold bricks or stone together. Mortar is made from sand, water, and lime.

muscle (MUHS uhl)
Part of the body that is made of strong fibers and that helps the body move.

nano- (NAN oh)
A billionth. A nanosecond is a billionth of a second.

oxygen (AHK suh junh)
A gas in the air that is necessary for life. It has no color, taste, or odor. Animals and people must breathe in oxygen to live.

patent (PAT uhnt)
A legal document that gives a person or company the right to be the only one who can make or sell an invention. It gives legal protection against someone stealing an inventor's idea.

phobia (FOH bee uh)
An extreme, abnormal fear of a certain place or thing.

planet (PLAN iht)
One of nine large heavenly bodies that orbit the sun.

pollen (PAHL uhn)
A fine, yellowish powder formed in the male parts of flowering plants. If the pollen is carried to a female part of a flower, seeds will form.

poltergeist (POHL tuhr gyst)
A ghost or spirit who makes tapping noises, slams doors, throws objects, or otherwise causes mischief.

pyramid (PEER uh mihd)
A solid having triangular sides meeting in a point. The Great Pyramid is a huge royal tomb built of stone by the ancient Egyptians.

relativity (rehl uh TIHV uh tee)
A theory, or idea, about such things as time, space, matter, and energy. The theory explains how these things are related to one another.

séance (SAY ahns)
A meeting of people trying to get in contact with the spirits of dead people. A séance is usually led by a person called a medium, who believes talking to the dead is possible.

slang (SLAYNG)
A casual kind of language that most people do not accept as proper English.

solar system (SOH luhr SIHS tuhm)
The sun and all the objects, such as planets, that move around it.

supernatural (soo puhr NACH uhr uhl)
Above or beyond what is natural.

supersonic (soo puhr SAHN ihk)
Faster than the speed of sound.

tomb (TOOM)
A grave or building in which a dead body is kept.

tuberculosis (too bur kyoo LOH sihs)
A disease that affects the lungs.

twitch (twihch)
A quick, jerking movement.

venom (VEHN uhm)
The poison of some snakes, spiders, and other animals.

volcano (vahl CAYN oh)
An opening in the surface of the earth through which lava, gases, and ashes are forced out.

Find Out More

There are so many exciting resources for you to use to learn all kinds of weird and wonderful facts. Pick a topic, then start your search. You'll find plenty to enjoy. The resources listed here are only a sampling. Your school or public library will have many more.

Ages 5-8

Hottest, Coldest, Highest, Deepest
by Steve Jenkins
(Houghton Mifflin, 1998)

Did you know that more than 1,200 inches of snow fell on Mount Rainier, in Washington State, in one year? Find out more about our natural world in this book.

How Do We Move?
by Carol Ballard
(Raintree, Steck-Vaughn, 1998)

Curious about how your body moves? This book tells you all about your bones, muscles, joints, nerves, and other parts of your body that help you move. Check out the other books in the How Your Body Works series.

I Didn't Know That Spiders Have Fangs and Other Interesting Facts About Arachnids
by Claire Llewellyn
(Copper Beech, 1997)

In this book you will learn many facts about spiders. Did you know that some spiders spit? Spitting spiders don't use webs.

Inspector McQ series
(World Book)

Kids love to ask questions. Inspector McQuestion, McQ to his friends, loves to answer them! This knowledgeable mouse leads ever-curious children on searches for answers to intriguing questions. Titles in the series include *All About You* and *All About Pets*.

My First Amazing World Explorer CD-ROM Activity Pack
on CD-ROM for Mac and Windows
(DK Multimedia, 1996)

This CD takes you on a fascinating trip around the world. It has more than 400 pop-ups packed with amazing facts on people, places, and wildlife. Have a great trip!

The True-or-False Book of Cats
by Patricia Lauber
(National Geographic Society, 1998)

Do you believe a cat can sense that an earthquake is going to happen? This book will give you the answer and lots more facts about cats.

Why Does Popcorn Pop? and Other Kitchen Questions
by Catherine Ripley
(Owl, 1997)

Find out why your stomach growls, why onions make you cry, and many other interesting facts about things that happen in the kitchen. Check out the other titles in the Questions and Answers Storybook series, too.

Ages 9 and Up

American Memory
Web site at http://rs6.loc.gov/

This American history collection contains documents, motion pictures, photographs, and sound recordings about important places and events in the history of the U.S. Browse or download!

Earth Explained: A Beginner's Guide to Our Planet
by Barbara Taylor
(Henry Holt, 1997)

In this title from the Your World Explained series, the author tells you the "whys" behind the facts about our Earth and the forces inside and outside of it. Future geologists and meteorologists won't want to miss this one.

Hidden Under the Ground: The World Beneath Your Feet
by Peter Kent
(Dutton, 1998)

There's a lot more going on underground than you would imagine! In this book, explore the world under your feet, from hidden rockets to underground cities and transportation systems.

Info Adventure series
(World Book)

These books are packed with facts and fantastic pictures that will amaze, amuse, and inform. Dramatic newspaper-style headlines, engaging text, and bold design give this series a distinct and appealing identity. Titles include *Daredevils, Great Mysteries, Super Heroes, Mega Machines, Olympic Gold,* and *Dangerous Animals.*

Junior Chronicle of the 20th Century
by Simon Adams
(DK, 1997)

Facts about all the great and not-so-great things that have happened over the past 100 years are in this book. From music to inventions to people—it's all here!

The New York Public Library Amazing Space: A Book of Answers for Kids

by Ann-Jeanette Campbell
(John Wiley, 1997)

Find answers to some of the most frequently asked questions about the universe. This book has fascinating stories about pulsars, supernovae, black holes, sunspots, and meteor showers.

Sports Illustrated for Kids

Web site at http://www.sikids.com

This Web site will give you current facts about the sports scene and will give you an opportunity to tell sports reporters what questions to ask athletes. You'll also be able to test your knowledge with this site's on-line trivia challenge.

The Unexplained Mysteries of the Universe

by Colin Wilson (DK, 1997)

In this book, you'll read about scary monsters, lost worlds, strange disappearances, and much more in this book of fascinating facts about the world's greatest mysteries. You'll want to take a look at the other titles in The Unexplained series, as well.

The Way Things Work 2.0

by David Macaulay
on CD-ROM for Mac and Windows
(DK Multimedia, 1998)

This award-winning CD describes over 200 machines in detail. You'll also learn many facts about the inventors.

World Book Looks At series

(World Book)

Find out fascinating and obscure facts about the subjects you like best in these 64-page books. Titles in the series include *The Age of Knights and Castles, Insects and Spiders, The American West, Inventions and Discoveries,* and *Wonders of the World.*

World Book Multimedia Encyclopedia

on CD-Rom for Mac and Windows
(World Book)

This general reference is loaded with information that will answer your questions and give you tons of new facts. You'll find thousands of photos and illustrations, videos, and animations.

Index

This index is an alphabetical list of important topics covered in this book. It will help you find information given in both words and pictures. To help you understand what an entry means, there is sometimes a helping word in parentheses, for example, **Aborigines** (people). If there is information in both words and pictures, you will see the words *with pictures* in parentheses after the page number. If there is only a picture, you will see the word *picture* in parentheses after the page number.

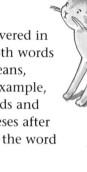

Illustration Acknowledgments

The publishers of *Childcraft* gratefully acknowledge the courtesy of illustrator **Steven Mach** and the following photographers, agencies, and organizations for the illustrations in this volume. When all the illustrations for a sequence of pages are from a single source, the inclusive page numbers are given. Credits should be read from left to right, top to bottom, on their respective pages. All illustrations are the exclusive property of the publishers of *Childcraft* unless names are marked with an asterisk (*).

12-13	© Mark Carwardine, Bruce Coleman Ltd.*
14-15	© Marc Van Roosmalen*; © Michel Peissel*; © George Schaller*
26-27	© Fritz Prenzel, Animals Animals*
28-29	© Zig Leszczynski, Animals Animals*; © J. Sommer Collection from, Archive Photos*
32-33	AP/Wide World*; University of Tasmania*; © Eastcott/Momatiuk, Earth Scenes*
34-35	© G.I. Bernard/OSF, Earth Scenes*; © OSF, Earth Scenes*
36-37	© Michael Fogden, Earth Scenes*
44-45	© Wernher Krutein, Liaison Agency*
50-51	© Tom Nebbia, Apsect Picture Library*; © Robert Aberman, Werner Forman Archive
52-53	U.S. Postal Service*
56-57	WORLD BOOK photo by David R. Frazier
60-61	E.M. Winkler, Stone: Properties, Durability in Man's Environment*
70-71	NASA*
78-79	© Edward S. Ross*; © Jonathan T. Wright, Bruce Coleman Inc.*; Corbis Images*
82-83	© Galen Rowell*
86-87	© Daniel Staquet, Liaison Agency*
88-89	© UPI/Corbis Images*; Air Force Flight Test Center History Office*
90-91	Itar-Tass/Sovfoto*; UPI/Corbis Images*
96-97	© World Book photo by Allan Landau
102-103	© Oliver Meckes/SPL from Photo Researchers*
106-107	© John Reader/SPL from Photo Researchers*
112-113	Liaison Agency*
114-115	AP/Wide World*; © Philip Plisson/Explorer from Photo Researchers*
116-117	Niesenbahn Tourism*; Honshu-Shikoku Bridge Authority*
120-121	UPI/Corbis Images*
124-125	© Dustin Carr & Harold Craighead, Cornell University*
126-127	© Louis Renault, Photo Researchers*
128-129	Seiko Epson Corporation*
138-139	Discovery Channel Eco-Challenge/photo by Dan Campbell*; © Vandystadt, Allsport*
140-141	The Children's Museum of Indianapolis*
156-157	St. Louis Post Dispatch*
160-161	© C.K. Lorenz, Photo Researchers*
164-165	Photofest*
166-167	AP/Wide World*
176-177	Dinodia Picture Agency*; MZTV Museum*
178-179	© Gaumont-Boreales, Liaison Agency*
180-181	© Twentieth Century Fox/Archive Photos*
182-183	WORLD BOOK photos by John R. Hamilton, Globe Photos
184-185	WORLD BOOK photos by John R. Hamilton, Globe Photos; Kelvin Jones for the motion picture "ANTZ" TM & © 1998 Dreamworks L.L.C., reprinted with permission by Dreamworks Animation*
192-193	© Ron Cohn, The Gorilla Foundation*
196-197	*Bison* by an unknown artist. 32,000 to 11,000 B.C. Altamira, Spain (SCALA/Art Resource)*; Logan Museum at Beloit College (Randall White)*
200-201	© Jack Vartoogian*
202-203	Corbis Images*
210-211	AP/Wide World*; © Craig Jones, Allsport*